**HBR'S 10 MUST READS**

The definitive
management ideas
of the year from
**Harvard Business Review.**

**2024**

HBR's 10 Must Reads series is the definitive collection of ideas and best practices for aspiring and experienced leaders alike. These books offer essential reading selected from the pages of *Harvard Business Review* on topics critical to the success of every manager.

**Titles include:**

HBR's 10 Must Reads 2015
HBR's 10 Must Reads 2016
HBR's 10 Must Reads 2017
HBR's 10 Must Reads 2018
HBR's 10 Must Reads 2019
HBR's 10 Must Reads 2020
HBR's 10 Must Reads 2021
HBR's 10 Must Reads 2022
HBR's 10 Must Reads 2023
HBR's 10 Must Reads 2024
HBR's 10 Must Reads for Business Students
HBR's 10 Must Reads for CEOs
HBR's 10 Must Reads for Executive Teams
HBR's 10 Must Reads for Mid-Level Managers
HBR's 10 Must Reads for New Managers
HBR's 10 Must Reads on AI
HBR's 10 Must Reads on AI, Analytics, and the New Machine Age
HBR's 10 Must Reads on Boards
HBR's 10 Must Reads on Building a Great Culture
HBR's 10 Must Reads on Business Model Innovation
HBR's 10 Must Reads on Career Resilience
HBR's 10 Must Reads on Change Management (Volumes 1 and 2)
HBR's 10 Must Reads on Collaboration
HBR's 10 Must Reads on Communication (Volumes 1 and 2)
HBR's 10 Must Reads on Creativity
HBR's 10 Must Reads on Design Thinking
HBR's 10 Must Reads on Diversity

The definitive
management ideas
of the year from
**Harvard Business Review.**

# 2024

**HARVARD BUSINESS REVIEW PRESS**
Boston, Massachusetts

Library of Congress Cataloging-in-Publication Data

Names: Harvard Business Review Press, editor.
Title: HBR's 10 must reads 2024 : the definitive management ideas of the
    year from Harvard Business Review.
Other titles: Harvard Business Review's ten must reads 2024 | HBR's 10
    must reads (Series)
Description: Boston, Massachusetts : Harvard Business Review Press, [2023] |
    Series: HBR's 10 must reads | Includes index.
Identifiers: LCCN 2023013157 (print) | LCCN 2023013158 (ebook) |
    ISBN 9781647825782 (paperback) | ISBN 9781647825799 (epub)
Subjects: LCSH: Success in business. | Industrial management. |
    Diversity in the workplace.
Classification: LCC HF5386 .H377 2024 (print) | LCC HF5386 (ebook) |
    DDC 650.1—dc23/eng/20230616
LC record available at https://lccn.loc.gov/2023013157
LC ebook record available at https://lccn.loc.gov/2023013158

ISBN: 978-1-64782-578-2
eISBN: 978-1-64782-579-9

# Contents

Every year a team of editors gathers to read and review, discuss and debate, 12 months' worth of *Harvard Business Review* articles to select the ones we think are most likely to spark conversation, inspire innovation, and move you and your organization forward. We bring to the (figurative) table our individual challenges and experiences, topic interests, and perspectives on the cutting-edge ideas driving business today. But we read and evaluate all the articles with *you* in mind. Keeping up with the latest research, trends, and influential thinking is time-consuming. If you're able to read only 11 articles, whether all at once on a flight or in stolen spurts during your day, which ones will bring you and your organization the most value? Which will surprise and delight you? Which will you talk about with friends and colleagues? Which will spur your thinking to action? We believe the articles in this collection meet those criteria.

The past few years have proved that one thing we know for certain is that nothing is certain. Our world is ever changing; we must work hard to adapt to whatever comes next while still trying to create and carry out long-term plans. Covid-19 is (mostly) behind us, yet its impact lingers: a dispersed and disengaged workforce, supply chain blips and breakdowns, and rusty interpersonal skills. We all endured the same global pandemic, yet it highlighted that our employees, customers, and businesses are in unique contexts that shape their worldview and ability to adjust to changing conditions. We made great technological strides, from switching to video for meetings to moving business into space, while watching enthusiasm for crypto swing from high to low. No bets are sure, and no one solution fits all. But we can learn new skills, revive stale connections, measure things that matter, and make headway despite headwinds. The articles in this collection will help you prepare for whatever lies ahead for you and your business.

Dealing with uncertainty and change is yet one more challenge for leaders, which is why we open this volume with **"Managers Can't Do It All."** With sweeping reengineering, digitization, agile initiatives, and the postpandemic move to remote work, the job description for "manager" has altered dramatically. Managers now have to think more about making their teams successful than about what individuals can do for them. They must coach performance rather than oversee tasks, and lead in rapidly changing environments. These additional responsibilities require managers to demonstrate new capabilities, and research shows that most of them are struggling to keep up. Some organizations, however, are heading off trouble by reimagining the manager's role. In this article Diane Gherson and Lynda Gratton look at three companies—Standard Chartered, IBM, and Telstra—that have helped managers develop new skills, rewire systems and processes to better support their work, and radically redefine their responsibilities to meet the new priorities of the era.

If you're not in tech, you may have asked yourself, **"What Is Web3?"** You've read the headlines and heard the buzz, but you may not be clear on what it is—and what it could do for you and your company. HBR editor Thomas Stackpole tackles this complicated and swiftly evolving subject and distills it, clearly explaining the differences among Web1, Web2, and Web3. His detailed case stories bring to life the challenges and the opportunities. We've also included "Cautionary Tales from Cryptoland," an interview with the software engineer and Web3 critic Molly White, to offset the headlines—and the hype.

The next article, **"Selling on TikTok and Taobao,"** continues the exploration of what tech could be, this time from a marketing perspective. Whether you remember watching QVC on TV or were raised on digital ads on tablets, you know that the future of retail lies in social commerce. Thomas S. Robertson, a professor of marketing at Wharton, provides case studies to inspire you to think about how your company might experiment with livestream commerce. To gain advantage, consider six key factors, including how to integrate it into your existing marketing strategy, how to select your key opinion leaders (aka influencers), and how to measure your success. Robertson explores what's behind the rise in livestream commerce, explains the motivations of brands that are already experimenting with it, and offers guidance on the smartest ways to invest in this emerging channel.

Weaving together the idea of customers as stakeholders and life in an uncertain and volatile world, **"Managing in the Age of Outrage"** addresses the polarization that is prevalent around the globe. Almost every leader in every sector must deal with angry stakeholders. But hearing employees or customers speak out over a singular incident is not a new phenomenon. What makes this era uniquely challenging is a perfect storm of three forces: People feel unhopeful about the future; they believe that the game has been rigged against them; and they are drawn to ideologies that legitimize an us-versus-them approach. In this piece Oxford's Karthik Ramanna shares a five-step framework for dealing with outrage that draws on analytical insights from disciplines as wide-ranging as the science of aggression, managerial economics, organizational behavior, and political philosophy.

From situations that feel difficult to manage to progress that feels difficult to measure, **"The Five Stages of DEI Maturity"** advances the diversity, equity, and inclusion (DEI) conversation. Companies looking to make progress on DEI begin with good intentions and often make big declarations about implementing ambitious strategies—before they have the necessary culture and structures in place to support their goals. Georgetown professor and organizational psychologist Ella F. Washington describes five stages that companies typically move through as they establish their DEI goals and work toward making progress on them. Understanding what stage your company is in can help you decide where to focus your energies most effectively and keep you from getting stuck. We've also added "To Avoid DEI Backlash, Focus on Changing Systems—Not People," by DEI strategist and consultant Lily Zheng, who recommends focusing on the process, policy, and practices that contribute to organizational inequity. Doing so will help galvanize your workforce while lowering the risk that your employees feel personally targeted.

We know that we measure what matters, but as with DEI efforts, context may make it difficult to gauge the impact of environmental, social, and governance (ESG) goals. Despite heightened attention to ESG issues, surprisingly few companies are making meaningful progress in delivering on their commitments. Why? Harvard Business School professor Mark R. Kramer and global social-impact consultant Marc W. Pfitzer argue in **"The Essential Link Between ESG Targets and Financial Performance"** that the key to building a sustainable business model is to tie your ESG goals to your business objectives, operations, and strategy. To integrate them into your company's core business models, you must identify the ESG issues material to your business; factor in ESG effects when making strategic, financial, and operational decisions; collaborate with stakeholders; redesign organizational roles; and communicate with investors. The rich examples in this article demonstrate that there are no easy answers and that ripples extend further than intended.

Meetings, especially those you have with your own manager or with your direct reports, are crucial to achieving your company's short- and long-term goals. But few organizations provide guidance or training on conducting individual meetings. And when our calendars are full, sometimes we shirk or shortchange our one-on-ones, believing that our time would be better spent elsewhere. Done right, however, these meetings add value. In **"Make the Most of Your One-on-One Meetings,"** author and professor Steven G. Rogelberg writes that managers should focus on making sure the meetings actually happen and at a predictable cadence, creating space for genuine conversation, asking good questions, offering support, and helping team members get what they need to thrive in both their short-term performance and their long-term growth. We've also included "Five Questions Every Manager Needs to Ask Their Direct Reports," by coach Susan Peppercorn, to provide additional suggested language and conversation starters that will make your employees feel seen and valued in your routine check-ins.

Intergenerational conflict isn't new, but with five generations in many workplaces, tensions are mounting. Lack of trust between older and younger workers often creates a culture of competition and resentment that leads to losses in productivity. But when age-diverse teams are managed well, their members can share a wide array of skills, knowledge, and networks with one another. **"Harnessing the Power of Age Diversity"** argues that today's organizations already have the means to help leaders take advantage of these assets. Megan W. Gerhardt, Josephine Nachemson-Ekwall, and Brandon Fogel, coauthors of the book *Gentelligence*, offer a four-part framework for identifying assumptions, adjusting your lens, taking advantage of differences, and embracing mutual learning. Alongside this piece we've added "Is Generational Prejudice Seeping into Your Workplace?" by Founders CEO Kristi DePaul and HBR editor Vasundhara Sawhney, which explores whether intergenerational anxiety stems from actual differences or is created by the mere belief that certain disparities exist.

Regardless of which generation you're in, **"The C-Suite Skills That Matter Most,"** by Raffaella Sadun, Joseph Fuller, Stephen Hansen, and PJ Neal, reveals another long-term impact of the pandemic—a shift in demand from candidates with strong technical skills to those with strong people skills. We need leaders who can motivate diverse, technologically savvy, and global workforces. The softer skills, including self-awareness, empathy, and the ability to listen and communicate well, are rarely recognized or fostered in the corporate world, especially at the senior-leader level. Companies still value C-suite executives with traditional administrative and operational skills. But they should increasingly be on the lookout for people with highly developed social skills—especially if their organizations are large, complex, and technologically intensive.

Moving forward when you're not sure what's next requires more than rethinking the hiring process; it requires rethinking business practices such as operations and innovation. If you think your organization or industry will *never* be in space or develop "bespoke launch services," think again. If your company gathers or uses GPS data, you're already getting value from space. And you're not alone. Rapidly falling costs and fleets of new satellites are creating big opportunities for business. Space is becoming a potential source of value for companies across a range of sectors, from agriculture to pharmaceuticals. In **"Your Company Needs a Space Strategy. Now,"** professors Matthew Weinzierl, Prithwiraj (Raj) Choudhury, Tarun Khanna, Alan MacCormack, and Brendan Rosseau propose four areas in which space could create value for your organization: data, capabilities, resources, and markets. Companies looking longer term will want to explore the value to be gained from conducting activities in space, utilizing space assets, and meeting demand from the new space age.

We close out this collection with **"Democratizing Transformation,"** by Harvard Business School professor Marco Iansiti and Microsoft chairman and CEO, Satya Nadella. If your company's digital transformation efforts seem to have sputtered or stalled, it's probably because the work cannot be done by isolated technologists and data scientists alone. True growth and transformation require that larger and more-diverse groups of employees—executives, managers, and frontline workers—come together to rethink how every aspect of your business should operate. The authors describe the five stages of digital transformation, from the traditional stage—in which digital and technology are strictly the province of the IT department—to the ideal, native stage. The hallmarks of the native stage are an operating architecture designed to deploy AI at scale across a huge, distributed spectrum of applications; a core of experts; broadly accessible, easy-to-use tools; and investment in training and capability-building across the enterprise.

We can't know, of course, what opportunities and challenges the coming year will bring. But we do know that we need to continue our work on initiatives that matter to our organizational culture and our planet (even when the goals are lofty and the metrics are fuzzy), that bridge divides of age and perspective, and that envision and create a future when the present is still a work in progress. In the absence of hard answers or road maps, we hope this curated collection gives you insights and inspiration to spark ideas for making strides toward the objectives that provide value for you and your organization.

—The Editors

HBR'S
10
MUST
READS

The definitive
management ideas
of the year from
**Harvard Business Review.**

**2024**

# Managers Can't Do It All

*by Diane Gherson and Lynda Gratton*

**JENNIFER STARES AT HER UPWARD-FEEDBACK REPORT** and wonders how she got to this point. How could a veteran like her, someone who was once celebrated as manager of the year, receive such negative ratings? She used to enjoy her role, but now everything feels out of control. Her job has been reshaped so constantly—by sweeping process reengineering, digitization, and agile initiatives, and most recently by remote work—that she always feels at least one step behind.

The amount of change that has taken place in just the past few years is overwhelming. The management layer above her was eliminated, which doubled the size of her team, and almost half the people on it are now working on cross-division projects led by *other* managers. She and her team used to meet in her office for progress reviews, but now she has no office, and if she wants to know how her people are doing, she has to join their stand-ups, which makes her feel like an onlooker rather than their boss. She no longer feels in touch with how everybody is doing, and yet she has the same set of personnel responsibilities as before: providing performance feedback, making salary adjustments, hiring and firing, engaging in career discussions.

Not only that, but she's being asked to take on even more. Because her company is rapidly digitizing, for example, she's responsible for upgrading her staff's technical skills. This makes her uncomfortable because it feels threatening to many of her team members. When she talks with them about it, she's expected to demonstrate endless amounts of empathy—something that has never been her strong suit. She's supposed to seek out diverse talent and create a climate of psychological safety while simultaneously downsizing the unit. She understands why all these things are important, but they're not what she signed up for when she became a manager, and she's just not sure that she has the emotional energy to handle them.

What happened to the stable, well-defined job that she was so good at for so long? What happened to the power and status that used to come with that job? Is *she* the problem? Is she simply no longer able to keep up with the demands of the evolving workplace? Is she now part of the "frozen middle"—the much-maligned layer of management that obstructs change rather than enables it?

Jennifer—a composite of several real people we have met in our work—has no answers to these questions. All she knows is that she's frustrated, unhappy, and overwhelmed.

As are managers everywhere.

One of us, Lynda, is an academic researcher and consultant to corporations, and the other, Diane, was until her recent retirement the chief human resources officer at IBM (in which she still owns stock). In those roles we have closely observed the changing job of the manager, and we can report that a crisis is looming.

The signs are everywhere. In 2021, when we asked executives from 60 companies around the world how their managers were doing, we got unanimous reports of frustration and exhaustion. Similarly, when the research firm Gartner asked 75 HR leaders from companies worldwide how their managers were faring, 68% reported that they were overwhelmed. Nonetheless, according to Gartner, only 14% of those companies had taken steps to help alleviate their managers' burdens.

The problem isn't hard to diagnose. The traditional role of the manager evolved in the hierarchical workplaces of the industrial age, but in our fluid, flatter, postindustrial age that role is beginning to look archaic.

The irony is that we actually need great people leaders more than ever. Microsoft has found, for example, that when managers help

# Idea in Brief

### The Problem

Managers are the lifeblood of organizations. In recent decades, as the workplace has changed, they've been asked to take on new responsibilities and demonstrate new skills—and are struggling to cope. This threatens productivity, employee well-being, and brand reputation.

### The New Reality

Change has come along three dimensions: power (managers have to think about making teams successful, not being served by them); skills (they're expected to coach performance, not oversee tasks); and structure (they have to lead in more fluid environments).

### The Way Forward

We need to do everything we can to help managers adapt. The three companies featured in this article have deliberately—and successfully—transformed the role of manager so that it better meets the demands of 21st-century work.

teams prioritize, nurture their culture, and support work-life balance, employees feel more connected and are more positive about their work. The consulting firm O.C. Tanner has likewise found that weekly one-to-ones with managers during uncertain times lead to a 54% increase in engagement, a 31% increase in productivity, a 15% decrease in burnout, and a 16% decrease in depression among employees. Meanwhile, according to McKinsey, having good relationships with their managers is the top factor in employees' job satisfaction, which in turn is the second-most-important determinant of their overall well-being.

Conversely, bad managers can significantly hurt retention and engagement: Seventy-five percent of the participants in the McKinsey survey reported that the most stressful aspect of their jobs was their immediate boss. As the saying goes, people join companies and leave their managers.

Something is clearly broken. If managers remain essential but their traditional role has become obsolete, then it's obviously time for a change.

In this article we'll make the case for redefining and even splitting the role rather than simply continuing to let it evolve, which is a potentially costly and disastrous course of action. But first let's briefly take stock of the waves of innovation that have brought us to this crisis point.

## Four Defining Business Movements

The first wave, *process reengineering,* began in about 1990 and lasted until the early 2000s. It focused on eliminating bureaucracy and boosting operational efficiencies. With the help of consulting firms, which developed practices around this kind of work, companies globalized and outsourced their processes, flattened their hierarchies, and in many cases put their remaining managers in "player-coach" roles that required them to take on workers' tasks. These changes reduced costs, but they also made life a lot harder for managers. They now had wider responsibilities and significantly larger teams to supervise and were also expected to dedicate themselves personally to projects and customers.

The next wave of innovation, *digitization,* arrived in about 2010. Promisingly, it democratized access to both information and people, but in doing so it undermined traditional sources of managerial power. CEOs and other senior leaders could now communicate directly with their entire workforces, sharing strategies, priorities, and important updates and responding to concerns. No longer a necessary part of the information loop, managers began to feel a loss of power, control, and status.

Then came the *agile movement* and its process changes, which companies began to adopt in the mid to late 2010s. It aimed to shorten timelines and turbocharge innovation by using internal marketplaces across whole organizations to match skills to work and to rapidly assemble project teams on an as-needed basis. As a result, managers started to lose touch with their reports, who now spent much of their time under the rotating supervision of the project managers they were temporarily assigned to. And because candidates could be matched to openings online, managers lost the power and authority involved with brokering career opportunities for their people.

Finally, a fourth wave arrived in 2020 with the pandemic, when companies and employees were forced to embrace the possibilities of *flexible work*. This was a watershed moment. It dramatically altered how and where work was done. Once employees were no longer tied to a physical workplace, managers lost the close control that they used to have over employees' performance and behavior—and employees began to realize that they could tap a greater range of job options, far beyond commuting distance from their homes. These changes were liberating, but they placed even more of a burden on managers—who now were also expected to cultivate empathetic relationships that would allow them to engage and retain the people they supervised.

These waves of innovation have changed the role of the manager along three dimensions: *power, skills*, and *structure*. In a power shift, managers have to think about making teams successful, not being served by them. In a skills shift, they're expected to coach performance, not oversee tasks; and in a structural shift, they have to lead in more fluid environments. (See the exhibit "From manager to people leader.")

These changes have empowered employees, which of course is a good thing. But they've also altered how managers drive productivity. Organizations are starting to recognize this. When we asked the executives in our 60-company survey to list the most important areas that managers need to focus on today, their top answers were coaching, communication, and employee well-being.

## New Models of Management

Some organizations have taken deliberate steps to reimagine the role of the manager. Let's take a look at transformative shifts that have been made at three very different companies in banking, tech, and telecommunications.

### Building new skills at scale

Most companies think of their top leaders as the people who make change happen—and are willing to spend millions on their

## From manager to people leader

*Three fundamental shifts in the role of managers today*

### A power shift: from "me" to "we"

| | | |
|---|---|---|
| My team makes me successful. | $\longrightarrow$ | I'm here to make my team successful. |
| I'm rewarded for achieving business goals. | $\longrightarrow$ | I'm also rewarded for improving team engagement, inclusion, and skills relevancy. |
| I control how people move beyond my unit. | $\longrightarrow$ | I scout for talent and help my team move fluidly to wider opportunities. |

### A skills shift: from task overseer to performance coach

| | | |
|---|---|---|
| I oversee work. | $\longrightarrow$ | I track outcomes. |
| I assess team members against expectations. | $\longrightarrow$ | I coach them to achieve their potential and invite their feedback on my management. |
| I provide work direction and share information from above. | $\longrightarrow$ | I supply inspiration, sensemaking, and emotional support. |

### A structural shift: from static and physical to fluid and digital

| | | |
|---|---|---|
| I manage an intact team of people in fixed jobs in a physical workplace. | $\longrightarrow$ | My team is fluid, and the workplace is digital. |
| I set goals and make assessments annually. | $\longrightarrow$ | I provide ongoing guidance on priorities and performance feedback. |
| I hold an annual career discussion focused on the next promotion. | $\longrightarrow$ | I'm always retraining my team and providing career coaching. |

development as a result. The layers of management below the top, the theory goes, are frozen in place and will resist change. But the executives at Standard Chartered—a retail bank, headquartered in London, with more than 750 branches in 50-plus countries—recently chose to think differently. Their 14,000 middle managers, they decided, would play a central role in the bank's growth.

Rather than wholly redesigning the job, the executive team began with some basic steps: changing the role's title, creating an accreditation process, and strengthening the sense of a managerial community. Managers became "people leaders," an acknowledgment of how important the human connection was in their work. Meanwhile, the new accreditation process evaluated future-focused capabilities such as driving growth, building trust, aligning teams, and making bold decisions. And the executive team worked to strengthen community by applying the local experiences of people leaders to problems across the whole company. For example, when in the course of filling 10 positions, one cohort of people leaders failed to hire anybody from an underrepresented group, the executive team didn't single the group out for criticism but instead seized the opportunity to ask the whole community, "How can we support you in making your teams more diverse?"

Next the executive team decided to focus on coaching, which has today become a crucial management skill. (See "The Leader as Coach," by Herminia Ibarra and Anne Scoular, HBR, November–December 2019.) Coaching, in fact, plays a key role in each of the three shifts we described earlier: When managers coach they're making a power shift by moving from instruction to support and guidance; a skills shift by moving from the oversight of work to the continual giving of feedback; and a structural shift by engaging with their people in a way that's dynamic and constant rather than static and episodic.

Standard Chartered had been working for decades on developing its top leaders into coaches. But now the challenge was scaling that effort up to 14,000 people leaders. The bank did this through a variety of initiatives—by using an AI-based coaching platform, for example, and by developing peer-to-peer and team coaching across all its markets in Africa, the Middle East, and Asia. It also launched a pilot project in which it offered to help people leaders pay for formal training and accreditation as coaches (by outside organizations approved by the global governing body for coaching). Those who accepted were expected to coach other employees; the goal was building what Tanuj Kapilashrami, the bank's head of human resources, describes as "a deep coaching culture." So many participants reported a boost in skills and confidence that the bank organized further rounds of training and accreditation, each of which was oversubscribed, with hundreds of people taking part around the world.

### Rewiring processes and systems

In 2013, as IBM's new chief human resources officer, Diane realized that to support the massive transformation that had been launched by then-CEO Ginni Rometty, the company needed a different kind of manager. IBM was changing 50% of its product portfolio over the next five years, moving into several growth businesses (among them the cloud, AI, cybersecurity, and blockchain), and migrating from software licensing to software as a service. At a worldwide town hall, Rometty announced that all employees would be required not only to develop new skills but also to learn to work differently. The company would build a culture optimized for innovation and speed—and needed its managers to lead retraining efforts, adapt their management styles to agile work methods, and get all employees engaged in the journey.

That meant doing three things: freeing managers up for additional responsibilities by digitally transforming their work; equipping them with new skills; and holding them accountable through a metrics-driven performance-development system. Their most important goal was employee engagement: Managers account for 70% of the variance in that metric.

The HR function deployed AI to eliminate administrative work, such as approving expense reports or transferring employees to a new unit. Personalized digital learning was introduced so that managers could access support on their mobile phones—for, say, just-in-time guidance on preparing for difficult conversations. New AI-driven programs also helped managers make better people decisions and spot issues like attrition risk. An AI-driven adviser has made it easier for managers to determine salary increases: It considers not only performance and market pay gaps but also internal data on employee turnover by skills, the current external demand for each employee's skills (scraped from competitor job postings), and the future demand.

Now when managers have salary conversations with employees, they can confidently share the rationale for their decisions, help team members understand the demand for their skills, and, most important, focus on supporting them as they build market-relevant capabilities and accelerate their career growth.

Like Standard Chartered, IBM also introduced an accreditation for managers, built on a new training curriculum. The impact has been significant: Managers who have obtained this accreditation are scoring five points higher today on employee engagement than those who have not.

In addition, IBM requires managers to get "licenses" in key activities by undergoing an in-house certification program. Licenses to hire, for example, are designed to ensure that managers select candidates in an objective and unbiased way, provide them with a well-designed experience, and ultimately make hires of high quality. The impact has been significant here too: Employees hired by licensed managers are 7% more likely to exceed expectations at six months and 45% less likely to leave the company within their first year than other hires are. Those numbers mean a lot in a company that makes more than 50,000 hires a year.

One major shift is the deliberate change from performance management to performance development. Not just about business results, the new system reflects the mindset and skills needed to manage in the modern workplace.

Feedback is at its core. Team members are asked whether their managers create an environment that encourages candid communication. Do they provide frequent and meaningful feedback? Do they help in the development of market-relevant skills? Are they effective career coaches? At the same time, HR gathers metrics on diversity and inclusion, regretted attrition, and skills development. The company then combines those metrics with its survey data and feeds the results into its Manager Success Index—a dashboard that allows managers to understand how well they're meeting expectations and to identify needs for both learning and "unlearning." Managers are invited to training programs on the basis of their specific development needs. Investing in these programs pays off: People who have completed at least one course in the past two years are 20% less likely to be in the bottom decile of the Manager Success Index, whereas those who have taken no leadership development courses are much more likely to be there.

IBM takes this idea seriously. Managers who do not demonstrate growth behaviors and who consistently underperform get moved out of managerial positions. The message to the company's managers is clear: Times have changed, and you must too. Your ongoing service as a manager is tightly connected to the continued growth and engagement of your people. We're here to support you in rethinking traditional practices, attitudes, and habits, and adopting ones better suited to new ways of working and the digital workplace.

### Splitting the role of the manager

Telstra, a $16 billion Australian telecommunications company that employs more than 32,000 people, has made perhaps the boldest move. When Telstra's CEO, Andy Penn, decided to make the company more customer-focused, fast-paced, and agile, he and his chief human resources officer, Alex Badenoch, dramatically flattened its hierarchy, reducing the number of organizational layers to three.

Penn, Badenoch, and their team recognized that the restructuring provided a perfect opportunity to redesign the managerial job. "This change has been needed for so long," Badenoch told us. "We realized we had to separate work and management and create two distinct roles: *leader of people* and *leader of work*." With very few exceptions, this new model applies to the entire organization.

Leaders of people are responsible for similarly skilled employees grouped into guildlike "chapters"—one for financial planners, say, and another for people experienced in change implementation. Most chapters consist of several hundred people, but some are larger. Subchapter leaders one level below are responsible for 15 to 20 members with narrower specializations and are located all over the world. What people do—not where they are—is what matters most.

Leaders of people ensure that the employees in their chapters have the skills and capabilities to meet the current and future needs of the business. They also help chapter members develop pathways to other chapters, to broaden insights and avoid silos. "The role of leaders of people," Badenoch told us, "is to know people beyond their work, to understand their career aspirations, to feed their minds and create thought provocations." Their performance is judged by such standards as how engaged they are with the people on their teams (measured by net promoter scores) and how well they fulfill requirements, among them the amount of time that their people are actively at work on projects, as opposed to being "on the bench."

Leaders of work focus on the flow of work and the commercial imperatives of the business. They don't directly manage people or control operating budgets. Instead, they create and execute work plans and determine which chapters to draw from for them. These leaders' performance is judged by such standards as the clarity of their planning, the quality of their estimates, and whether their projects are on time and on budget. (See the sidebar "Telstra's Dual Manager Model.")

This bold experiment has been widely acclaimed internally. "You actually get two people out of it who are dedicated to your development," one employee commented. "Your chapter lead [leader of people] is there to talk to you about your growth, and you get to have some great, powerful conversations about the type of work you want to do and how to get there. You can be very honest and share your aspirations openly with them. They have an amazing network and can get you assignments that allow you to explore different roles. And your project leader [leader of work] is there on a day-to-day basis to provide you direction on the work you need to do and on the business outcomes that we're trying to deliver."

At Telstra neither group of leaders is subordinate to the other. Their pay ranges are the same, and they participate as equals in the senior leadership team. Together they determine what Badenoch calls "the equation of work," which reveals "who is performing well, and what the skill and capacity is." Leaders of people have a sense of

# Telstra's Dual Manager Model

**TO BETTER COPE** with what it calls the new "equation of work," the telecommunications firm Telstra has flattened its hierarchy and split the traditional role of manager into two jobs: one devoted to people and the other to process. The two types of managers are equals and coordinate closely with each other.

| Leader of people | Leader of work |
| --- | --- |
| Leads a global chapter of employees with similar skills | Leads an agile project team drawn from chapters and external contractors |
| Owns the talent capacity, including personnel budgets | Owns the work, including project plans and budgets |
| Forecasts skills gaps and closes them through training and hiring | Forecasts demand for skills |
| Selects employees for projects | Bids for employees |
| Is responsible for employee engagement, career movement, and skills | Is responsible for project deliverables and business outcomes |

the dynamics of their talent pool, and leaders of work have a sense of the dynamics of workflow. By coordinating with their counterparts, leaders of people can anticipate skills gaps and prioritize training investments, or forecast undercapacity and the need for hiring—all while being mindful of the commitments, health, and well-being of employees.

This bifurcated model of management isn't new. It's been used for years in consulting, where one often finds a division between practice leadership and project leadership. What is new here is the context. Telstra has proven that the model can work effectively and profitably across all functions in big companies that have adopted agile practices and flexible work arrangements.

---

Let's step back and consider where we are. For roughly a century our approach to management was conventionally hierarchical. That made sense because work was organized sequentially and in silos, jobs were fixed, workspaces were physical, and information flowed downward. But that's no longer the case. In today's world of work, enabled by digitization, we prioritize agility, innovation, responsiveness, speed, and the value of human connection. All of that demands the new approach to management that we've discussed: one that involves shifts in power, skills, and structure.

We have to get this right. At no time in the past has the investor community paid such close attention to human capital in corporations—checking Glassdoor for signals of toxic work environments, demanding disclosure of metrics such as diversity and employee turnover. As the stewards of culture, managers are the lifeblood of organizations. The current state of overwhelmed, confused, and underskilled managers creates significant risk, not just to productivity and employee well-being but also to brand reputation.

Sometimes it takes a jolt like the new titles at Telstra and Standard Chartered, or the Manager Success Index at IBM, to signal that change is afoot. But in all cases the march to sustainable behavioral change is long. The Telstra experience shows us the benefits of a radical new organizational design, and the Standard Chartered and IBM experiences show us that at a minimum companies can take deliberate steps to shift managers' mindsets, energy, and focus. With these kinds of actions—which institutionalize change—we can ensure that people get the leadership they need in the new world of work.

**Originally published in March–April 2022. Reprint** R2202F

# What Is Web3?

*by Thomas Stackpole*

DO YOU REMEMBER THE FIRST TIME YOU heard about Bitcoin? Maybe it was a faint buzz about a new technology that would change everything. Perhaps you felt a tingle of FOMO as the folks who got in early suddenly amassed a small fortune—even if it wasn't clear what the "money" could legitimately be spent on (really expensive pizza?). Maybe you just wondered whether your company should be working on a crypto strategy in case it *did* take off in your industry, even if you didn't really care one way about it or the other.

Most likely, soon after Bitcoin came to your attention—whenever that may have been—there was a crash. Every year or two, bitcoin's value has tanked. Each time it does, skeptics rush to dismiss it as dead, railing that it was always a scam for nerds and crooks and was nothing more than a fringe curiosity pushed by techno-libertarians and people who hate banks. Bitcoin never had a future alongside *real* tech companies, they'd contend, and then they'd forget about it and move on with their lives.

And, of course, it would come back.

Bitcoin now seems to be everywhere. Amidst all the demands on our attention, many of us didn't notice cryptocurrencies slowly seeping into the mainstream. Until suddenly Larry David was pitching them during the Super Bowl; stars like Paris Hilton, Tom Brady, and Jamie Foxx were hawking them in ads; and a frankly terrifying Wall Street–inspired robot bull celebrating cryptocurrency was unveiled in Miami. What was first a curiosity and then a speculative niche has become big business.

Crypto, however, is just the tip of the spear. The underlying technology, blockchain, is what's called a "distributed ledger"—a database hosted by a network of computers instead of a single server—that offers users an immutable and transparent way to store information. Blockchain is now being deployed to new ends: for instance, to create "digital deed" ownership records of unique digital objects—or nonfungible tokens. NFTs have exploded in 2022, conjuring a $41 billion market seemingly out of thin air. Beeple, for example, caused a sensation last year when an NFT of his artwork sold for $69 million at Christie's. Even more esoteric cousins, such as DAOs, or "decentralized autonomous organizations," operate like headless corporations: They raise and spend money, but all decisions are voted on by members and executed by encoded rules. One DAO recently raised $47 million in an attempt to buy a rare copy of the U.S. Constitution. Advocates of DeFi (or "decentralized finance," which aims to remake the global financial system) are lobbying Congress and pitching a future without banks.

The totality of these efforts is called "Web3." The moniker is a convenient shorthand for the project of rewiring how the web works, using blockchain to change how information is stored, shared, and owned. In theory, a blockchain-based web could shatter the monopolies on who controls information, who makes money, and even how networks and corporations work. Advocates argue that Web3 will create new economies, new classes of products, and new services online; that it will return democracy to the web; and that is going to define the next era of the internet. Like the Marvel villain Thanos, Web3 is inevitable.

Or is it? While it's undeniable that energy, money, and talent are surging into Web3 projects, remaking the web is a major undertaking. For all its promise, blockchain faces significant technical, environmental, ethical, and regulatory hurdles between here and hegemony. A growing chorus of skeptics warns that Web3 is rotten with speculation, theft, and privacy problems, and that the pull of centralization and the proliferation of new intermediaries is already undermining the utopian pitch for a decentralized web.

## Idea in Brief

Web3 is being touted as the future of the internet. The vision for this new blockchain-based web includes cryptocurrencies, NFTs, DAOs, decentralized finance, and more. It offers a read/write/own version of the web, in which users have a financial stake in and more control over the web communities they belong to. Web3 promises to transform the experience of being online as dramatically as PCs and smartphones did. It is not, however, without risk. Some companies have entered the space only to face a backlash over the environmental impact and financial speculation (and potential for fraud) that comes with Web3 projects. And while blockchain is offered as a solution to privacy, centralization, and financial exclusion concerns, it has created new versions of many of these problems. Companies need to consider both the risks and the benefits before diving in.

Meanwhile, businesses and leaders are trying to make sense of the potential—and pitfalls—of a rapidly changing landscape that could pay serious dividends to organizations that get it right. Many companies are testing the Web3 waters, and while some have enjoyed major successes, several high-profile firms are finding that they (or their customers) don't like the temperature. Most people, of course, don't even really know what Web3 is: In a casual poll of HBR readers on LinkedIn in March 2022, almost 70% said they didn't know what the term meant.

Welcome to the confusing, contested, exciting, utopian, scam-ridden, disastrous, democratizing, (maybe) decentralized world of Web3. Here's what you need to know.

### Install Update: From Web1 to Web3

To put Web3 into context, let me offer a quick refresher.

In the beginning, there was the internet: the physical infrastructure of wires and servers that lets computers, and the people in front of them, talk to each other. The U.S. government's ARPANET sent its first message in 1969, but the web as we know it today didn't emerge until 1991, when HTML and URLs made it possible for users to navigate between static pages. Consider this the read-only web, or Web1.

In the early 2000s, things started to change. For one, the internet was becoming more interactive; it was an era of user-generated content, or the read/write web. Social media was a key feature of Web2 (or Web 2.0, as you may know it), and Facebook, Twitter, and Tumblr came to define the experience of being online. YouTube, Wikipedia, and Google, along with the ability to comment on content, expanded our ability to watch, learn, search, and communicate.

The Web2 era has also been one of centralization. Network effects and economies of scale have led to clear winners, and those companies (many of which are listed above) have produced mind-boggling wealth for themselves and their shareholders by scraping users' data and selling targeted ads against it. This has allowed services to be offered for "free," though users initially didn't understand the implications of that bargain. Web2 also created new ways for regular people to make money, such as through the sharing economy and the sometimes lucrative job of being an influencer.

There's plenty to critique in the current system: The companies with concentrated or near-monopoly power have often failed to wield it responsibly, consumers who now realize that they *are* the product are becoming increasingly uncomfortable with ceding control of their personal data, and it's possible that the targeted-ad economy is a fragile bubble that does little to actually boost advertisers. As the web has grown up, centralized, and gone corporate, many have started to wonder whether there's a better future out there.

Which brings us to Web3. Advocates of this vision are pitching it as a roots-deep update that will correct the problems and perverse incentives of Web2. Worried about privacy? Encrypted wallets protect your online identity. About censorship? A decentralized database stores everything immutably and transparently, preventing moderators from swooping in to delete offending content. Centralization? You get a real vote on decisions made by the networks you spend time on. More than that, you get a stake that's *worth something.* You're not a product—you're an owner. This is the vision of the read/write/own web.

## OK, but What *Is* Web3?

The seeds of what would become Web3 were planted in 1991, when scientists W. Scott Stornetta and Stuart Haber launched the first blockchain—a project to time-stamp digital documents. But the idea didn't really take root until 2009, when Bitcoin was launched in the wake of the financial crisis (and at least partially in response to it) by the pseudonymous inventor Satoshi Nakamoto. It and its under-girding blockchain technology work like this: Ownership of the cryptocurrency is tracked on a shared public ledger, and when one user wants to make a transfer, "miners" process the transaction by solving a complex math problem, adding a new "block" of data to the chain and earning newly created bitcoin for their efforts. While the Bitcoin chain is used just for currency, newer blockchains offer other options. Ethereum, which launched in 2015, is both a cryptocurrency and a platform that can be used to build other cryptocurrencies and blockchain projects. Gavin Wood, one of its cofounders, described Ethereum as "one computer for the entire planet," with computing power distributed across the globe and controlled nowhere. Now, after more than a decade, proponents of a blockchain-based web are proclaiming that a new era—Web3—has dawned.

Put *very* simply, Web3 is an extension of cryptocurrency, using blockchain in new ways to new ends. A blockchain can store the number of tokens in a wallet, the terms of a self-executing contract, or the code for a decentralized app (dApp). Not all blockchains work the same way, but in general, coins are used as incentives for miners to process transactions. On "proof of work" chains like Bitcoin, solving the complex math problems necessary to process transactions is energy-intensive by design. On a "proof of stake" chain, which are newer but increasingly common, processing transactions simply requires that the verifiers with a stake in the chain agree that a transaction is legit—a process that's significantly more efficient. In both cases, transaction data is public, though users' wallets are identified only by a cryptographically generated address. Blockchains are "write only," which means you can add data to them but can't delete it.

Web3 and cryptocurrencies run on what are called "permission-less" blockchains, which have no centralized control and don't require users to trust—or even know anything about—other users to do business with them. This is mostly what people are talking about when they say blockchain. "Web3 is the internet owned by the builders and users, orchestrated with tokens," says Chris Dixon, a partner at the venture capital firm a16z and one of Web3's foremost advocates and investors, borrowing the definition from Web3 adviser Packy McCormick. This is a big deal because it changes a foundational dynamic of today's web, in which companies squeeze users for every bit of data they can. Tokens and shared ownership, Dixon says, fix "the core problem of centralized networks, where the value is accumulated by one company, and the company ends up fighting its own users and partners."

In 2014, Ethereum's Wood wrote a foundational blog post in which he sketched out his view of the new era. Web3 is a "reimagination of the sorts of things we already use the web for, but with a fundamentally different model for the interactions between parties," he said. "Information that we assume to be public, we publish. Information that we assume to be agreed, we place on a consensus ledger. Information that we assume to be private, we keep secret and never reveal." In this vision, all communication is encrypted, and identities are hidden. "In short, we engineer the system to mathematically enforce our prior assumptions, since no government or organization can reasonably be trusted."

The idea has evolved since then, and new use cases have started popping up. The Web3 streaming service Sound.xyz promises a better deal for artists. Blockchain-based games, like the Pokémon-esque Axie Infinity, let users earn money as they play. So-called stablecoins, whose value is pegged to the dollar, the euro, or some other external reference, have been pitched as upgrades to the global financial system. And crypto has gained traction as a solution for cross-border payments, especially for users in volatile environments.

"Blockchain is a new type of computer," Dixon tells me. Just like it took years to understand the extent to which PCs and smartphones transformed the way we use technology, blockchain has been in a long incubation phase. Now, he says, "I think we might be in the golden period of Web3, where all the entrepreneurs are entering." Although the eye-popping price tags, like the Beeple sale, have garnered much of the attention, there's more to the story. "The vast majority of what I'm seeing is smaller-dollar things that are much more around communities," he notes, like Sound.xyz. Whereas scale has been a key measure of a Web2 company, engagement is a better indicator of what might succeed in Web3.

Dixon is betting big on this future. He and a16z started putting money into the space in 2013 and invested $2.2 billion in Web3 companies last year. He is looking to double that in 2022. The number of active developers working on Web3 code nearly doubled in 2021, to roughly 18,000—not huge, considering global numbers, but notable nonetheless. Perhaps most significantly, Web3 projects have become part of the zeitgeist, and the buzz is undeniable.

But as high-profile, self-immolating startups like Theranos and WeWork remind us, buzz isn't everything. So what happens next? And what should you watch out for?

## What Web3 Might Mean for Companies

Web3 will have a few key differences from Web2: Users won't need separate log-ins for every site they visit but instead will use a centralized identity (probably their crypto wallet) that carries their information. They'll have more control over the sites they visit, as they earn or buy tokens that allow them to vote on decisions or unlock functionality.

It's still unclear whether the product lives up to the pitch. Predictions as to what Web3 might look like at scale are just guesses, but some projects have grown pretty big. The Bored Ape Yacht Club (BAYC), NBA Top Shot, and the cryptogaming giant Dapper Labs have built successful NFT communities. Clearinghouses such as Coinbase (for buying, selling, and storing cryptocurrency) and OpenSea (the largest digital marketplace for crypto collectibles and NFTs) have created Web3 on-ramps for people with little to no technical know-how.

While companies such as Microsoft, Overstock, and PayPal have accepted cryptocurrencies for years, NFTs—which have recently exploded in popularity—are the primary way brands are now experimenting with Web3. Practically speaking, an NFT is some mix of a deed, a certificate of authenticity, and a membership card. It can confer "ownership" of digital art (typically, ownership is recorded on the blockchain and a link points to an image somewhere) or rights or access to a group. NFTs can operate on a smaller scale than coins because they create their own ecosystems and require nothing more than a community of people who find value in the project. For example, baseball cards are valuable only to certain collectors, but that group *really* believes in their value.

Most successful forays by traditional companies into Web3 have been ones that create communities or plug in to existing ones. Consider the NBA: Top Shot was one of the first NFT projects from a legacy brand, and it offered fans the opportunity to buy and trade clips, called "moments" (a LeBron James dunk, for instance), that function like trading cards. It took off because it created a new kind of community space for fans, many of whom may have already been collecting basketball cards. Other front-runner brands, such as Nike, Adidas, and Under Armour, similarly added a digital layer to their existing collector communities. All three companies offer NFTs that can be used in the virtual world—for example, allowing the owner to gear up an avatar—or that confer rights to products or exclusive streetwear drops in the real world. Adidas sold $23 million worth of NFTs in less than a day and instantly created a resale market on OpenSea, just like what you might see after a limited drop of new shoes. Similarly, *Time* magazine launched an NFT project to build an online community that leverages the publication's deep history.

Bored Ape Yacht Club is the biggest success story of an NFT project going mainstream. Combining hype and exclusivity, BAYC offers access to real-life parties and online spaces, along with usage rights to the ape's image—further reinforcing the brand. An ape NFT puts the owner in an exclusive club, both figuratively and literally.

One lesson from these efforts is that on-ramps matter, but less so the more committed the community is. Getting a crypto wallet isn't hard, but it is an added step. So Top Shot doesn't require one—users can just plug in their credit card—which helped it acquire interested users new to NFTs. The Bored Ape Yacht Club was a niche interest, but when it took off, it became a catalyst for people to create wallets and drove interest in OpenSea.

Some companies have had rockier experiences with NFT projects and crytpo features. For example, when Jason Citron, the CEO of Discord, a voice, video, and text communication service, teased a feature that could connect the app to crypto wallets, Discord users mutinied, leading him to clarify that the company had "no current plans" to launch the tie-in. The underwear brand MeUndies and the UK branch of the World Wildlife Fund both quickly pulled the plug on NFT projects after a fierce backlash by customers furious about their sizable carbon footprint. Even the success stories have hit bumps in the road. Nike is currently fighting to have unauthorized NFTs "destroyed," and OpenSea is full of knockoffs and imitators. Given that blockchain is immutable, this is raising novel legal questions, and it isn't clear how companies will handle the issue. Further, there's recent evidence that the market for NFTs is stalling entirely.

Companies who are considering stepping into this space should remember this: Web3 is polarizing, and there are no guarantees. Amid many points of disagreement, the chief divide is between people who believe in what Web3 *could* be and critics who decry the many problems dogging it right now.

## System Error: The Case Against Web3

The early days of a technology are a heady time. The possibilities are endless, and there's a focus on what it can do—or *will* do, according to optimists. I'm old enough to remember when the unfettered discourse enabled by Twitter and Facebook was supposed to sow democracy the world over. As Web3's aura of inevitability (and profitability) wins converts, it's important to consider what could go wrong and recognize what's *already* going wrong.

### It's rife with speculation

Skeptics argue that for all the rhetoric about democratization, ownership opportunities, and mass wealth building, Web3 is nothing more than a giant speculative economy that will mostly make some already-rich people even richer. It's easy to see why this argument makes sense. The top 0.01% of bitcoin holders own 27% of the supply. Wash trading, or selling assets to yourself, and market manipulation have been reported in both crypto and NFT markets, artificially pumping up value and allowing owners to earn coins through sham trades. In an interview on the podcast *The Dig*, reporters Edward Ongweso Jr. and Jacob Silverman characterized the whole system as an elaborate upward transfer of wealth. Writing in *The Atlantic*, investor Rex Woodbury called Web3 "the financialization of everything" (and not in a good way). On a more granular level, Molly White, a software engineer, created Web3 Is Going Just Great, where she tracks the many hacks, scams, and implosions in the Web3 world, underscoring the pitfalls of the unregulated, Wild West territory.

The unpredictable, speculative nature of the markets may be a feature, not a bug. According to technologist David Rosenthal, speculation on cryptocurrencies is the engine that drives Web3—that it can't work without it. "[A] permissionless blockchain *requires* a cryptocurrency to function, and this cryptocurrency *requires* speculation to function," he said in a talk at Stanford in early 2022. Basically, he's describing a pyramid scheme: Blockchains need to give people something in exchange for volunteering computing power, and cryptocurrencies fill that role—but the system works only if other people are willing to buy them believing that they'll be worth more in the future. Stephen Diehl, a technologist and vocal critic of Web3, floridly dismissed blockchain as "a one-trick pony whose only application is creating censorship-resistant crypto investment schemes, an invention whose negative externalities and capacity for harm vastly outweigh any possible uses."

### The tech isn't practical (and it's expensive)

Questions abound as to whether Web3—or blockchain, really— makes sense as the technology that will define the web's next era. "Whether or not you agree with the philosophy/economics behind cryptocurrencies, they are—simply put—a software architecture disaster in the making," says Grady Booch, chief scientist for software engineering at IBM Research. All technology comes with trade-offs, Booch explained in a Twitter Spaces conversation, and the cost of a "trustless" system is that it's highly inefficient, capable of processing only a few transactions per minute—tiny amounts of data compared with a centralized system like, say, Amazon Web Services. Decentralization makes technology more complicated and further out of reach for basic users, rather than simpler and more accessible.

While it's possible to fix this by adding new layers that can speed things up, doing so makes the whole system more centralized, which defeats the purpose. Moxie Marlinspike, founder of the encrypted messaging app Signal, put it this way: "Once a distributed ecosystem centralizes around a platform for convenience, it becomes the worst of both worlds: centralized control, but still distributed enough to become mired in time."

Right now, the inefficiency of blockchain comes at a cost, quite literally. Transaction costs on Bitcoin and Ethereum (which calls them gas fees) can run anywhere from a few bucks to hundreds of dollars. Storing one megabyte of data on a blockchain distributed ledger can cost thousands, or even tens of thousands, of dollars—yes, you read that correctly. That's why the NFT you bought probably isn't actually on a blockchain. The code on the chain indicating your ownership includes an address, pointing to where the image is stored. Which can and has caused problems, including your pricy purchase disappearing if the server it *actually* lives on goes down.

### It enables harassment and abuse

The potential for disastrous unintended consequences is very real. "While blockchain proponents speak about a 'future of the web' based around public ledgers, anonymity, and immutability," writes Molly White, "those of us who have been harassed online look on in horror as obvious vectors for harassment and abuse are overlooked, if not outright touted as features." Although crypto wallets theoretically provide anonymity, the fact that transactions are public means that they can be traced back to individuals. (The FBI is pretty good at doing this, which is why crypto isn't great for criminal enterprise.)

"Imagine if, when you Venmo-ed your Tinder date for your half of the meal, they could now see every other transaction you'd ever made," including with other dates, your therapist, and the corner store by your house. That information in the hands of an abusive ex-partner or a stalker could be life-threatening.

The immutability of the blockchain also means that data can't be taken down. There's no way to erase anything, whether it's a regrettable post or revenge porn. Immutability also could spell major problems for Web3 in some places, such as Europe, where the General Data Protection Regulation (GDPR) enshrines the right to have personal data erased.

### It's currently terrible for the environment

Web3's environmental impact is vast and deeply damaging. It can be broken into two categories: energy use and tech waste, both of which are products of mining. Running a network that depends on supercomputers competing to solve complex equations every time you want to save data on a blockchain takes a tremendous amount of energy. It also generates e-waste: According to Rosenthal, Bitcoin produces "an average of one whole MacBook Air of e-waste per 'economically meaningful' transaction" as miners cycle through quantities of short-lived computer hardware. The research he bases this claim on, by Alex de Vries and Christian Stoll, found that the annual e-waste created by Bitcoin is comparable to the amount produced by a country the size of the Netherlands.

Whether and how these issues will be addressed is hard to say, in part because it's still unclear whether Web3 will really catch on. Blockchain is a technology in search of a real use, says technology writer Evgeny Morozov. "The business model of most Web3 ventures is self-referential in the extreme, feeding off people's faith in the inevitable transition from Web 2.0 to Web3." Tim O'Reilly, who coined "Web 2.0" to describe the platform web of the early 2000s, claims that we're in an investment boom reminiscent of the dot-com era before the bottom fell out. "Web 2.0 was not a version number; it was the second coming of the web after the dot-com bust," he says. "I don't think we're going to be able to call Web3 'Web3' until after the crypto bust. Because only then will we get to see what's stuck around."

If that's true, then innovation is going to come at significant cost. As Hilary Allen, an American University law professor who studies the 2008 financial crisis, points out, the system now "mirrors and magnifies the fragilities of shadow banking innovations that resulted in the 2008 financial crisis." If the Web3 bubble bursts, it could leave a lot of folks high and dry.

## Early Days Are Here Again

So, where exactly is Web3 headed? Ethereum cofounder Vitalik Buterin has expressed concerns about the direction his creation has taken but continues to be optimistic. In a response to Marlinspike on the Ethereum Reddit page, he conceded that the Signal founder presented "a correct criticism of the *current state* of the ecosystem" but maintained that the decentralized web is catching up, and pretty quickly at that. The work being done now—creating libraries of code—will soon make it easier for other developers to start working on Web3 projects. "I think the properly authenticated decentralized blockchain world is coming and is much closer to being here than many people think."

For one, proof of work—the inefficient-by-design system Bitcoin and Ethereum run on—is falling out of vogue. Instead of mining, which uses intensive amounts of energy, validation increasingly comes from users buying in (owning a stake) to approve transactions. Ethereum estimates that the update to proof of stake will cut its energy usage by 99.95%, while making the platform faster and more efficient. Solana, a newer blockchain that uses proof of stake and "proof of history," a mechanism that relies on time stamps, can process 65,000 transactions per second (compared with Ethereum's current rate of about 15 per second and Bitcoin's seven) and uses about as much energy as two Google searches—consumption it buys carbon offsets for.

Some companies are adopting a hybrid approach to blockchain, which offers the benefits without the constraints. "There are a lot of really interesting new architectures, which put certain things on the blockchain but not others," he tells me. A social network, for instance, could record your followers and who you follow on the blockchain, but not your posts, giving you the option to delete them.

Hybrid models can also help companies address GDPR and other regulations. "To comply with the right to erasure," explain Cindy Compert, Maurizio Luinetti, and Bertrand Portier in an IBM white paper, "personal data should be kept private from the blockchain in an 'off-chain' data store, with only its evidence (cryptographic hash) exposed to the chain." That way, personal data can be deleted in keeping with GDPR without affecting the chain.

For better or worse, regulation is coming—slowly—and it will define the next chapter of Web3. China has banned cryptocurrencies outright, along with Algeria, Bangladesh, Egypt, Iraq, Morocco, Oman, Qatar, and Tunisia. Europe is considering environmental regulations that would curb or ban proof-of-work blockchains. In the U.S., the Biden administration issued an executive order in March 2022 directing the federal government to look into regulating cryptocurrencies.

With so much of Web3 still being hashed out, it remains a high-risk, high-reward bet. Certain companies and sectors have more incentive than others to try their luck, particularly those that got burned by being left out in earlier eras of the web. It's not a coincidence that a media company like Time is interested in the opportunities of Web3 after Web2 decimated its business model. Other organizations—like Nike and the NBA, which already have experience with limited drops and commoditizing moments—may have simply found that their business models are an easy fit. Other businesses won't have as clear a path.

The soaring claims around Web3—that it will take over the internet, upend the financial system, redistribute wealth, and make the web democratic again—should be taken with a grain of salt. We've heard all this before, and we've seen how earlier episodes of Web3 euphoria fizzled. But that doesn't mean it should be written off entirely. Maybe it booms, maybe it busts, but we'll be living with some form of it either way. What version—and how your company responds—could determine the future of the digital economy and what life online looks like for the next internet epoch. For now, that future is still up for grabs. Nothing, after all, is inevitable.

———————

# Cautionary Tales from Cryptoland

*An interview with Molly White by Thomas Stackpole*

All of a sudden, it feels like Web3 is everywhere. The money, the buzz, the *name* all make it seem like Web3 will inevitably be the next big thing. But is it? And do we even want it to be?

As the hype has reached a fever pitch, critics have started to warn of unintended and overlooked consequences of a web with a blockchain backbone. And while Web3 advocates focus on what the future of the internet *could* be, skeptics such as Molly White, a software developer and Wikipedia editor, are focused on the very real problems of the here and now.

White created the website Web3 Is Going Just Great, a time line that tracks scams, hacks, rug pulls, collapses, shady dealings, and other examples of problems with Web3. HBR.org spoke to White over email about what people aren't hearing about Web3, how blockchain could make internet harassment much worse, and why the whole project might be "an enormous grift that's pouring lighter fluid on our already-smoldering planet." This interview has been lightly edited.

*You make it very clear that you don't have a financial stake in Web3 one way or another. So what led you to start your project and write about Web3's problems?*

**Molly White:** Late 2021 was when I really began to notice a huge shift in how people talk about crypto. Instead of being primarily used for speculative investments by people who were willing to take on a lot of risk in exchange for hopes of huge returns, people began to talk about how the whole web was going to shift toward services that were built using blockchains. Everyone would have a crypto wallet, and everyone would adopt these new blockchain-based projects for social networks, video games, online communities, and so on.

This shift got my attention, because until then crypto had always felt fairly "opt-in" to me. It was previously a somewhat niche technology, even to software engineers, and it seemed like the majority of people who engaged with it financially were fairly aware of the volatility risks. Those of us who didn't want anything to do with crypto could just not put any money into it.

Once crypto began to be marketed as something that everyone would need to engage with, and once projects began trying to bring in broader, more mainstream audiences—often people who didn't seem to understand the technology or the financial risks—I got very concerned. Blockchains are not well suited to many, if not most, of the use cases that are being described as "Web3," and I have a lot of concerns about the implications of them being used in that way. I also saw just an enormous number of crypto and Web3 projects going terribly: people coming up with incredibly poorly thought-out project ideas and people and companies alike losing tons of money to scams, hacks, and user error.

*In the examples you've collected, what are some of the common mistakes or misapprehensions you see in companies' efforts to launch Web3 projects, whether they're NFTs (non-fungible tokens) or something else?*

My overwhelming feeling is that Web3 projects seem to be a solution in search of a problem. It often seems like project creators knew they wanted to incorporate blockchains somehow and then went casting around for some problem they could try to solve with a blockchain without much thought as to whether it was the right technology to address it, or even if the problem was something that could or should be solved with technology at all.

Kickstarter might have been the most egregious example of this: Late last year they announced, much to the chagrin of many in their user base, that they would be completely rebuilding their platform on a blockchain. In an interview to explain the decision, COO Sean Leow gave the distinct impression that he had no idea why they were reimplementing their platform this way—what governance problems they were trying to solve, why a blockchain would be effective in solving them.

Companies also seem to announce NFT projects without doing much research into how these have gone for other companies in their sector. We've seen enough NFT announcements by video game studios that have gone so badly that they've chosen to reverse the decision within days or even hours. And yet somehow a new game company will do this and then be surprised at the backlash over NFTs' considerable carbon footprint or the sense that they're just a grift. The same is true for ostensibly environmentally conscious organizations announcing NFTs—even in some cases projects that are entirely focused on environmentalism, like the World Wildlife Fund, which tried and failed to launch a less carbon-intensive NFT series.

I firmly believe that companies first need to identify and research the problem they are trying to solve, and *then* select the right technology to do it. Those technologies may not be the latest buzzword, and they may not cause venture capitalists to come crawling out of the woodwork, but choosing technologies with that approach tends to be a lot more successful in the long run—at least, assuming the primary goal is to actually solve a problem rather than attract VC [venture capital] money.

*One of the most surprising (to me, anyway) arguments you make is that Web3 could be a disaster for privacy and create major issues around harassment. Why? And does it feel like the companies "buying into" Web3 are aware of this?*

Blockchains are immutable, which means once data is recorded, it can't be removed. The idea that blockchains will be used to store user-generated data for services like social networks has enormous implications for user safety. If someone uses these platforms to harass and abuse others, such as by doxing, posting revenge pornography, uploading child sexual abuse material, or doing any number of other very serious things that platforms normally try to thwart with content-moderation teams, the protections that can be offered to users are extremely limited. The same goes for users who plagiarize artwork, spam, or share sensitive material like trade secrets. Even a user who themself posts something and then later decides they'd rather not have it online is stuck with it remaining on-chain indefinitely.

Many blockchains also have a very public record of transactions: Anyone can see that a person made a transaction and the details of that transaction. Privacy is theoretically provided through pseudonymity—wallets are identified by a string of characters that aren't inherently tied to a person. But because you'll likely use one wallet for most of your transactions, keeping one's wallet address private can be both challenging and a lot of work and is likely to only become more challenging if this future vision of crypto ubiquity is realized. If a person's wallet address is known and they are using a popular chain like Ethereum to transact, anyone [else] can see all transactions they've made.

Imagine if you went on a first date, and when you paid them back for your half of the meal, they could now see every other transaction you'd ever made—not just the public transactions on some app you used to transfer the cash but *any* transactions: the split checks with all of your previous dates, that monthly transfer to your therapist, the debts you're paying off (or not), the charities to which you're donating (or not), the amount you're putting in a retirement account (or not). What if they could see the location of the corner store by your apartment where you so frequently go to grab a pint of ice cream at 10 p.m.? And this would also be visible to your ex-partners, your estranged family members, your prospective employers, or any number of outside parties interested in collecting your data and using it for any purpose they like. If you had a stalker or had left an abusive relationship or were the target of harassment, the granular details of your life are right there.

There are some blockchains that try to obfuscate these types of details for privacy purposes. But there are trade-offs here: While transparency can enable harassment, the features that make it possible to achieve privacy in a trustless system also enable financial crimes like money laundering. It is also very difficult to use those currencies (and to cash them out to traditional forms of currency). There are various techniques that people can use to try to remain anonymous, but they tend to require technical skill and quite a lot of work on the user's end to maintain that anonymity.

*This point of view seems almost totally absent from the conversation. Why do you think that is?*

I think a lot of companies haven't put much thought into the technology's abuse potential. I'm surprised at how often I bring it up and the person I'm talking to admits that it's never crossed their mind.

When the abuse potential is acknowledged, there's a very common sentiment in the Web3 space that these fundamental problems are just minor issues that can be fixed later, without any acknowledgment that they are intrinsic characteristics of the technology that can't easily be changed after the fact. I believe it's completely unacceptable to release products without any apparent thought to this vector of user risk, and so I am shocked when companies take that view.

*One of the mainstays of the pitch made by Web3 proponents is that blockchain can democratize (or re-democratize) the web and provide new sources of wealth and opportunity—even banking the unbanked. What's your take on that?*

It's a compelling pitch; I'll give them that. But crypto has so far been enormously successful at taking wealth from the average person or the financially disadvantaged and "redistributing" it to the already wealthy. The arguments I've seen for how this same technology is suddenly going to result in the democratization of wealth have been enormously uncompelling. The emerging crypto space is very poorly regulated, especially the newer parts of it pertaining to decentralized finance. It's difficult for me to see a future where poorly regulated technology with built-in perverse financial incentives will magically result in fairer, more accessible systems.

As for "banking the unbanked" and the democratization of the web, people are falling into a trap that technologists have fallen into over and over again: trying to solve social problems purely with technology. People are not unbanked because of some technological failure. People lack access to banking services for all sorts of reasons: They don't have money to open a bank account to begin with, they're undocumented, they don't have access to a physical bank or an internet or mobile connection, or they don't trust banks due to high levels of corruption in their financial or judicial systems.

These are not problems that can be solved solely through the addition of a blockchain. Indeed, crypto solutions introduce even *more* barriers: the technological know-how and the level of security practices required to safeguard a crypto wallet; the knowledge and time to try to distinguish "scammy" projects from those that are trying to be legitimate; the lack of consumer protections if something happens to an exchange where you are keeping your funds; and the added difficulty of reversing fraud when it does occur.

In my view, the places where crypto has done some good—and I do openly acknowledge that it has done some good—have primarily been in situations where there are enormous societal and political failings, and *any* replacement is better than what exists. For example, some people have successfully used crypto to send remittances to people under oppressive regimes. These examples are fairly limited, and the fact that it's worked seems largely because crypto hasn't been deployed in such a widespread way for those regimes to try to become involved.

### Given all of this, what do you think is the cultural draw of Web3?

The ideological argument for Web3 is very compelling, and I personally hold many of the same ideals. I *strongly* believe in working toward a more equitable and accessible financial system, creating a fairer distribution of wealth in society, supporting artists and creators, ensuring privacy and control over one's data, and democratizing access to the web. These are all things you will hear Web3 projects claiming to try to solve.

I just don't think that creating technologies based around cryptocurrencies and blockchains is the solution to these problems. These technologies build up financial barriers; they don't knock them down. They seek to introduce a layer of financialization to everything we do that I feel is, in many ways, worse than the existing systems they seek to replace. These are social and societal issues, not technological ones, and the solutions will be found in societal and political change.

### Should HBR.org even be doing this package on Web3? Are we buying into—or amplifying—the hype cycle?

I think we are comfortably beyond the "ignore it and hope it goes away" phase of crypto. I know I decided I was beyond that phase late last year. I think the best thing that journalists who report on crypto can do at this stage is ask the tough questions, seek out experts wherever they can, and try not to fall for the boosterism.

Crypto and Web3 are complex on so many levels—technologically, economically, sociologically, legally—that it is difficult for any single person to report on all issues, but there are extremely competent people who have examined crypto through each of these lenses and who are asking those tough questions.

One of the biggest failures of the media in reporting on crypto has been uncritically reprinting statements from crypto boosters with little reflection on the legitimacy or feasibility of those statements. It doesn't have to be that way. That is not to say that there needs to be a double standard, either—I think most, if not all, crypto skeptics welcome pushback and critical editing of what they say and write (though I do think the financial incentive to be skeptical of crypto is dwarfed compared to the incentive to be positive about it).

Kevin Roose recently suggested in "The Latecomer's Guide to Crypto" in the Sunday *New York Times* that, in the Web 2.0 era, the early skeptics were to blame for the ills of social media because they weren't "loud enough" in their skepticism. I would counter that they were not given the opportunity to be as loud as they wanted to be and that those who did hear them did not listen, or at least did not meaningfully act upon what they heard. Perhaps there is an opportunity for history not to repeat itself.

Originally published on hbr.org, May 10, 2022. Reprint BG2202

# Selling on TikTok and Taobao

*by Thomas S. Robertson*

AS FASHION SHOWS GO, the one that took place on Facebook Live in April 2021 was unique. The first model to strut down the catwalk was Cindy, a seven-month-old puppy wearing a green-and-blue canine flotation device. Next up was Mandalay, a tan dog wearing a fleece hoodie with built-in backpack. The omnichannel team at Petco, headed by chief marketing officer Katie Nauman, organized the livestream event, which highlighted canine outfits from two of its house brands. Each item modeled was featured prominently at the bottom of the screen. "If you see something you like, you can just click it and immediately make your purchase," the host explained. "Get your wallets ready!"

Consumers responded. The event, which lasted just 22 minutes, drew 200,000 live viewers; six months later, nearly 1 million people had watched clips from the show. Sales from the event were twice the cost of producing it; engagement was 2.6 times higher than organizers had expected; and all seven models (provided by a rescue shelter) were adopted afterward. The doggy fashion show was Petco's first foray into livestream commerce but not its last: Three months later, a livestreamed sports competition for dogs, Petco Field Day, drew 2.4 million viewers and generated twice the return on investment as the fashion show did.

In the 1980s the QVC and HSN cable channels, together with a host of infomercial producers, demonstrated the power of selling on television. Over the past decade the format has migrated to the internet, where online streaming video that offers the ability to purchase in real time—or *livestream commerce*—is fast becoming the medium of choice. Today brands can sell via video on a host of platforms, such as YouTube Live, Instagram Live, LinkedIn Live, Facebook Live, Twitch, Twitter, and TikTok.

In China, where Alibaba's Taobao platform provides an app that integrates product demonstration with the ability to purchase instantly, the livestream commerce market hit 1.2 trillion yuan (roughly $200 billion) in 2020, accounting for 10% of the online shopping market. It is projected to account for as much as 20% to 25% of online sales in 2023, according to iResearch China. In the United States, livestream commerce accounted for $6 billion in sales in 2020 and $11 billion in 2021, and growth is increasing dramatically: Revenues in 2023 are projected to reach $26 billion, according to Statista.

In the United States, livestream commerce has proven particularly attractive to beauty and fashion brands. At Nordstrom, for instance, 50% of livestream events were beauty focused in 2021. But a growing range of companies are also beginning to offer products and services via livestream, including Ferragamo and Cartier in luxury goods, Lowe's in home improvement, and Walmart in multiple product categories. Walmart's entry in particular illustrates how established brands are embracing livestream commerce as a way to build consumer engagement and present a modern, innovative image to customers. One sign of the format's potential: Although Walmart has some 4,700 U.S. stores and more than 10,000 worldwide, its chief marketing officer, William White, says, "The future of retail lies in social commerce." Walmart is scheduled to run more than 100 livestream events in 2022, up from 30 in 2021.

In this article I explore the forces propelling the rise of livestream commerce, explain the motivations of brands experimenting with the format, and offer guidance to companies as they consider the smartest ways to invest in this emerging channel.

# Idea in Brief

In China, livestream commerce—selling products via live video on platforms such as Taobao and TikTok—will account for as much as 20% to 25% of online sales in 2023. In the United States, it accounted for $11 billion in sales in 2021, and growth is increasing dramatically. It's no wonder brands as diverse as Nordstrom, Petco, and Walmart are embracing the format. This article explains why consumers are so drawn to livestream commerce and what's motivating companies to use it. No single company has yet cracked the code for livestream-channel success, but the author lays out lessons from early successes, including which type of platform to choose, how to select influencers, and how to measure your efforts.

## What's Driving Livestream Commerce

In a typical livestream-commerce event, the consumer watches product demonstrations presented by influencers (also called hosts or creators and referred to as KOLs, or "key opinion leaders," in China). Hosts are chosen for their personality, influence, or knowledge (or a combination of those factors), and they help to make the experience entertaining for participants.

Some of the excitement around the livestream format stems from its embrace of video. Research has shown that video achieves greater engagement than does text or still photography. Now that traditional e-commerce is a quarter-century old, consumers find it boring. It's becoming difficult for more static websites to generate much enthusiasm, particularly among Gen Z and younger Millennial consumers. Yes, young people still buy from Amazon—but so do their parents and grandparents. It's not surprising that they prefer a fresher alternative.

The ubiquity of smartphones and the dominance of social media are also drivers. In study after study, social media is found to have the greatest influence on the buying patterns of Gen Z consumers, with Millennials not far behind. Social media sites are designed to be sticky, and many are designed for, or work well with, livestream commerce. In China, for example, the sheer dominance of Taobao

Live guarantees a sizable audience when a company hosts a livestream event. Although most of the large U.S. social-media platforms are embracing livestream commerce, the favored format seems to be TikTok, the short-form platform featuring user-generated video and owned by China-based ByteDance. TikTok has the advantage of being designed for video, whereas other platforms are being retrofitted to accommodate video. People express themselves on TikTok through dance, comedy, tutorials, and wherever else their imagination takes them. Its demographics are young—41% of users are between the ages of 16 and 24, and 90% of those users open the app daily. That means there's always an audience for brands to sell to on TikTok.

Livestream commerce also creates a sense of community. While traditional online shopping is solitary, livestream commerce has a communal feel—similar to watching the Super Bowl. Consumers are able to see and be seen in what might be thought of as a meaningful social moment. Moreover, they can gain social currency with friends for attending a novel event. Or they may develop friendships by participating in livestream events. TikTok, for instance, uses an algorithm to connect people with similar interests. QVC, as it has morphed beyond cable to include livestream commerce, now has dedicated YouTube channels that seek to connect people with overlapping interests—whether in beauty, jewelry, food, or home furnishings. When consumers feel that they are among "friends," they have a more pleasurable shopping experience. Feeling a sense of community may also help buyers to rationalize their purchases, because affirmation is perceived or confirmed when they buy the same things that others are buying. Social imitation is a powerful force.

That is why influencers are so essential to livestream commerce. Marketers have always known the value of personal influence. It is often cited by consumers as the most important reason for a purchase. Today's opinion leaders may have millions of followers. Walmart's U.S. Holiday 2020 livestream commerce event on TikTok featured Michael Le, an influencer with approximately 50 million followers, in a variety show featuring national and private-label fashion brands for sale.

## What's in It for Companies

An obvious reason companies are embracing livestream commerce is to drive short-run revenue, but it's not the only one. According to interviews with executives at a range of companies experimenting with the format, there are five main objectives: generate immediate sales, reach new consumer segments, introduce new products, educate consumers, and create buzz.

### Generate immediate sales

A boost to short-run sales is usually the objective for low-commitment products and services—those that are not too expensive or complicated. Indeed, much of the success of the Taobao Live platform in China comes from livestreaming in these product categories. Events can be surprisingly informal and improvised: Some 60% of Taobao Live sessions are broadcast from stores and use sales associates as the demonstrators and KOLs. Taobao executives like to say that all you need in order to sell on their platform is a camera and a mobile phone. Similarly, in the United States, Nordstrom has had success with livestream shopping events hosted by store employees. These efforts represent true online/offline integration and a new form of the omnichannel approach.

### Reach new consumer segments

Livestream is most popular with members of Gen Z and younger Millennials—attractive target markets for many brands. As Daniella Vitale, Ferragamo's North America CEO, points out, the demographics for most luxury brands skew older, yet the brands must reach younger consumers to build their future success. To do that, Vitale's team selects celebrities and influencers and arranges TikTok events that run on influencers' channels, since those sites are considered "more authentic" than a channel owned by the brand.

### Introduce new products

Livestream commerce has produced some dramatic results for companies launching new products. Jimmy Choo, for example, has had substantial success in Asia launching sneakers at high price points. Helene Phillips, Jimmy Choo's senior vice president, tells of success using KOLs on a livestream commerce event that reached 16 million eyeballs and sold 300 pairs of sneakers in minutes on Tmall. That may not seem like high demand, but as Phillips explains, scarcity is critical for luxury products: "You want to sell out quickly, and you can't be too available."

### Educate consumers

Livestreaming is a powerful means of not only making consumers aware of product alternatives or categories but also teaching consumers how to use a product. Lowe's runs livestream commerce events to educate viewers on product usage and to drive online sales. Livestream fashion shows introduce consumers to new styles and encourage sales during the runway event. Livestream cooking demonstrations give participants the ability to purchase ingredients or utensils. Albertsons, the mega supermarket chain, has run its own successful livestream commerce events using the Firework platform. A more direct form of education occurs when consumers can livestream with a sales associate in the store. Using an app such as Hero, a consumer can chat with a sales associate who can explain a product and send photos.

### Create buzz

When done well, livestream commerce events generate buzz thanks to their novelty, the sense of community they can build, and the excitement the hosts create. Mark Yuan, the cofounder of Wonder Live Shopping, a livestream commerce platform in beta testing, explains that when consumers develop a habit of accessing the same influencer channel on the app site, they become loyal to the host and that community. A successful livestream event can lead to more sales after the event—largely owing to word of mouth. This cascade effect depends on the product category: Fashion and luxury brands, for instance, may provide a high social value to consumers who share them with friends and acquaintances. The higher hedonic value of such brands creates more positive emotions that lead to buzz. Alternatively, buzz may be a natural outcome of a passionate enthusiast community. The startup Whatnot focuses on collector and enthusiast audiences and, according to CEO Grant LaFontaine, when viewers have a great experience, they talk about it because it becomes part of their identity.

## A Guide for Companies

Particularly in the United States, livestream commerce is still an experimental channel, and no single company has yet cracked the code. As your company begins experimenting with it, here are the key factors to consider.

### Integrate it into your marketing strategy

Companies will follow different paths to achieve livestream commerce success. But the first principle for all of them is that livestream must be part of the overall marketing strategy. Livestream is not an independent marketing vehicle—it's just a new channel. What is presented on livestream must be compatible with product line plans, brand positioning, and overall communication objectives.

For many companies, livestream commerce is proving particularly effective as a way to build rapid awareness and to try out new products or test new markets. Because the focus is on immediate purchases, customers tend to buy more quickly while watching a livestream event than when browsing in a store. Amanda Baldwin, CEO of Supergoop!, says that when it launched in China, livestream commerce gave the brand immediate visibility, which is atypical for a brand of its size just starting out.

After an event, other elements of marketing strategy come into play to generate repeat purchases and long-term loyalty. Social media, direct mail, and advertising build and extend customer engagement to generate (more) buzz and reach additional customers.

### Recognize the learning curve

As with any new go-to-market vehicle, success won't happen instantly, and managers must ask questions to fine-tune their approach. Are we reaching the correct audience? Are we using the right technology? Is the content appropriate for the audience? Executives conducting livestream commerce events generally say that their first efforts were suboptimal but that they learned from them and built successful processes for future events. "It can't just be a camera in a store," says Ferragamo's Vitale. "Production values are critical to reflect the status of luxury brands." Brands in various product categories will learn different lessons from their initial forays.

### Run livestream events when there is news

Novelty or newness is highly correlated with sales success. Offering a special product available only during the livestream is one way to create novelty. Newness can be created by seasonality—marking holidays or special times of year like back to school. Many brands build their livestream commerce schedule around holidays that are meaningful for their product categories. This sort of promotion planning is familiar territory to most brands. Nordstrom Senior VP Fanya Chandler suggests that brands should identify a regular cadence for livestream commerce events so that consumers can plan when to attend.

### Select optimal platforms

Many players are racing to build livestream commerce solutions. Retailers have a range of options to choose from.

*Native social platforms,* such as TikTok, Instagram, Facebook, and YouTube, are layering new functionality for livestream commerce into their existing platforms, hoping to capitalize on their massive audiences.

*Marketplace platforms,* such as Amazon, are building livestream capabilities (such as Amazon Live) into their existing e-commerce infrastructure to give buyers and sellers a new way to interact. Additionally, startups such as Whatnot and NTWRK are building marketplace platforms with the objective of providing a seamless experience for buyers and sellers to make transactions within a livestream video format, similar to Taobao in China.

*Licensed software providers,* such as CommentSold, Bambuser, and Firework, are enabling companies to run livestream commerce events on their own websites and apps, giving companies more control over their customers' experiences and data.

Although all three approaches hold promise, competition is intense, and each has its own challenges. Social media platforms have the advantages of reach and scale, but their ad-based business models and natively social tech design are inhibitors to optimizing the livestream experience for consumers. Alternatively, e-commerce marketplaces are more tailored to selling and therefore may be better positioned to integrate livestream commerce. But Amazon, at least, has famously prioritized efficiency over user experience on its site. Marketplace startups are laser-focused on experience and capturing communities of enthusiasts to gain traction, but they must scale their double-sided marketplaces (brands and consumers) rapidly to win adequate share. Lastly, licensed software allows for companies to embrace livestream commerce while closely controlling the experience and resulting data, but this approach limits reach to audiences already engaged on their own websites.

For companies, the choice of platform is largely driven by which market segments are the priority, because the different platforms have different demographics. Consideration also must be given to the typical content featured on the platforms. NTWRK, for example, is particularly strong in streetwear and gaming, and might be the right choice for brands operating in that space.

### Select your influencers wisely

There should be a match between the brand's persona and the persona of the influencer. Brands utilizing more than one platform may need to choose a variety of influencers. The size of the influencer's following is, of course, a significant variable. Brands should ask, What number of consumers is the influencer likely to bring to the livestream event? There is some debate among companies as to the value of macro versus micro influencers. The latter may deliver fewer numbers, but customers may consider them to be more authentic. That quality is particularly relevant in product categories where genuine expertise is valued.

### Measure your livestream success

When making livestream commerce commitments, companies must track four metrics: audience size, audience engagement, short-run sales, and long-run impact.

When it comes to *audience size*, bigger is usually better, but it depends on the breadth of the market segment you are trying to reach and whether the product has mass appeal. The bias for most companies is to reach larger audiences via livestream. Traditional forms of marketing are then used to build awareness for upcoming livestream events to drive future attendance.

*Audience engagement* can be measured during the event by the quantity and quality of interaction between audience members and the host. On most livestream platforms, viewers have the ability to comment, to ask questions about the product, and to register "likes." After the event, companies may also track Net Promoter Scores. Greater engagement levels are assumed to signal a more positive customer sentiment toward the product and the host, and brands can gather meaningful data from this real-time feedback.

The ultimate benefit of livestream commerce is the consumer's ability to purchase items in real time without leaving the stream. Thus, *sales* during the event are an obvious performance metric. Companies predict sales for a livestream event by setting a target conversion rate given the size of the audience and conversion experiences from previous events.

The *long-term impact* of livestream events is harder to define, but similar to other marketing campaigns that generate buzz, it may be tracked in part by social media comments and coverage in mass media. And although livestream commerce does tend to shorten the customer journey when compared with other selling environments, companies should recognize that viewers who have not purchased today may still be interested in their products. So when measuring the long-term impact, brands should understand that viewers of livestream events may convert to customers at a later date. There-fore, marketers will need to find ways to create ongoing connections with livestream viewers.

---

Livestream commerce is at an inflection point in the United States. Marketing executives have been creating their own road maps, experimenting and investing in livestream commerce as part of their integrated marketing strategies. To gain early-mover advantage and reap network effects, companies need to start early, learn fast, and build large audiences before competitors can make significant inroads. The spoils will go to the companies that get it right quickly.

**Originally published in September–October 2022.  Reprint** S22053

# Managing in the Age of Outrage

*by Karthik Ramanna*

**LEADERS IN EVERY SECTOR ARE NOW DEALING** with angry stakeholders. Witness the crisis confronting government officials in Ottawa in early 2022, when the city was blockaded by large numbers of Freedom Convoy truckers protesting Covid-19 vaccination requirements. At the same time, customers and the media were pressuring GoFundMe, TD Bank, and others to cut off donations to the protesters. Even a low-key organization can find itself suddenly coping with outrage from both employees and external stakeholders.

Managing angry stakeholders is nothing new. What sets apart the times we live in is a perfect storm of three forces. First, many people feel unhopeful about the future, for reasons ranging from climate change to demographic shifts to wage stagnation. Whatever the cause, they believe the future will be worse than the present. Second, they often feel—whether rightly or wrongly—that the game is rigged and they have been treated unfairly. Consider, for instance, reports that the wealthiest often pay taxes at lower rates than the middle class does, or evidence of systemic bias in the opportunities available to minorities. Third, many people are being drawn, perhaps as a result of the first two forces, to ideologies of "othering"—that is, away from Enlightenment liberalism and toward an us-versus-them approach. The historian Samuel Huntington called this "the clash of civilizations."

In this article I offer a framework for managing stakeholder outrage that draws on analytical insights from disciplines as wide-ranging as the science of aggression, managerial economics, organizational behavior, and political philosophy. It forms the basis of a course I teach at Oxford, "Managing in the Age of Outrage," and has been built inductively through deep-dive case studies on organizations from multiple sectors, including IKEA, the London Metropolitan Police, Nestlé, and Oxford University Hospitals. The framework has five steps: *turning down the temperature, analyzing the outrage, shaping and bounding your responses, understanding your power to mobilize others,* and *renewing resilience.* Some steps are relatively complex, others fairly simple, but all involve a good measure of common sense, and nothing that follows should be wildly revelatory to seasoned managers. The value of the framework lies in its consolidation of insights.

## Step 1: Turning Down the Temperature

This step involves two actions. The first is simply acknowledging the clinical bases of outrage. The second is observing processes for engagement that stakeholders have ideally agreed upon *in advance of* situations that raise the temperature.

### Clinical bases of outrage

The behavioral science of aggression is a voluminous field. A key managerial insight is that the interplay of ambient conditions, emotions, and cognitive reasoning shapes the mind's response to situations.

To begin with, the science shows that physical environment matters: We are more likely to lose our tempers in a hot and humid room than in a well-ventilated one. Next, we know that when our cognitive-reasoning resources are limited, emotions are likely to drive our actions. A busy or distracted brain tends to react emotionally, and thus aggressively (as part of a fight-or-flight response), in a crisis. Hence the advice to "sleep on" charged decisions, to allow time for reflection. An emotional response is not

## Idea in Brief

Almost every leader in every sector is now dealing with angry stakeholders. Even a revered company like Apple can find itself suddenly managing outrage flashpoints, both with employees and with external groups. Such encounters are nothing new; what sets this time apart is a perfect storm of three forces: (1) Many people feel unhopeful about the future; (2) many feel, rightly or wrongly, that the game has been rigged against them; and (3) many are being drawn toward ideologies that legitimize an us-versus-them approach. The author offers a five-step framework for dealing with outrage that draws on analytical insights from disciplines as wide-ranging as the science of aggression, managerial economics, organizational behavior, and political philosophy. It forms the basis of a course he teaches at Oxford and has been built inductively through a series of deep-dive case studies on a variety of organizations, including IKEA, the London Metropolitan Police, Nestlé, and Oxford University Hospitals.

always bad, but our cognitive faculties should be given time to process an initial one.

Finally, research suggests that we interpret events through mental "scripts"—heuristics for how we think the world works. These scripts are developed from and reinforced by prior experiences, and even seemingly irrational scripts may become part of our cognitive response. For instance, repeated exposure to biased narratives on social media can influence scripts over time, contributing to outrage.

### Shared processes

Providing comfortable ambient conditions for debate and time for reflection on initial emotional impulses is relatively straightforward. But what can you do about differing scripts? Given that you have no control over the experiences that have shaped an individual's deep-seated script, it is best to avoid directly challenging it. You may not see it as legitimate, but you are unlikely to change it—certainly not in one sitting. You can, however, create a nonthreatening space where your stakeholders can explicitly render their scripts. Doing so can be cathartic and a first step toward building an understanding on which sustainable solutions rest.

One of my responsibilities at Oxford's Blavatnik School of Government is to convene public leaders from more than 60 jurisdictions (including China and the United States, India and Pakistan, Israel and Palestine, Russia and Ukraine) to build coalitions on divisive issues such as climate change, migration, and inequality. Diverging scripts are endemic to our setting.

To keep our community functioning and even thriving, we have developed and agreed in advance on our rules of engagement. That is crucial, because you cannot seek legitimacy for a process you are already using to address a contentious issue. As a manager, you should take the time to identify your key stakeholders and seek their commitment before you get into firefighting mode.

Our community rules are simple: No one may claim that a script is too offensive to be heard, but all must be accountable for how their words land on others. That second point sets up community members to aspire to be leaders rather than simply debaters. It prompts all stakeholders to temper their communications, not in self-censorship but with the hope of gradually helping others understand (even if not agree with) their worldview. And by encouraging community members to share their scripts in the context of their own biases, we are more likely to generate collective decisions that withstand the passage of time.

## Step 2: Analyzing the Outrage

Sharing and reflecting on scripts across your stakeholder community takes you to the second step, which also has two parts.

### Causal analysis

In June 2020, as London emerged from a three-month lockdown, Cressida Dick, the commissioner of the London Metropolitan Police, faced backlash from Black Londoners who, it was revealed, had been subject to the Met's heavy use of stop and search at a rate four times that of other groups. Dick, much of her own force, and victims of (rising) crime saw stop and search as a useful deterrent, but many

Black residents of the city wanted the policy ended. Protesters pointed out that this group was more likely to be in essential service operations and thus more likely to be on the streets during lockdown. Since the rates of actual arrest were similar across demographics, there seemed little reason to "target" Blacks. Activists therefore demanded that Dick acknowledge that the Met was "institutionally racist."

In responding to a situation like that, you need to identify which of the three drivers of outrage is in play: despair about the future, feeling that the game has been rigged, or an ideology of othering? Managers have some scope for engaging with the first two: They can provide reasons to become more hopeful about the future, and they may be able to address why stakeholders feel cheated. For example, anger at the Met's lockdown use of stop and search could be examined in the context of Londoners' long history of experiencing policing as biased against minorities. Official reports had criticized such practices as far back as 1981 and 1999. That history provided Dick with a starting point: To build trust with disenchanted citizens, her actions would need to at least improve on the Met's responses from 20 years prior.

But if the outrage can be traced to ideologies of othering, avoid direct engagement. It risks throwing fuel on the fire, diminishing the prospect of a resolution. That was the mistake government officials made during the Freedom Convoy blockade in Ottawa. They realized that although some truckers had defensible political demands, others saw the protests as a means to achieve exclusionary social ends. By taking on those ideologies and branding the truckers as "racists," the officials only inflamed the protesters (inviting more racists to the melee) and reduced the potential for negotiating an end to the blockade (because they could not be seen as doing business with racists).

My point here is not to deny managers their personal ideologies (and right to be offended) but to caution that direct engagement with stakeholders over ideological differences is unlikely to be effective. Avoiding such battles keeps a polarizing situation from escalating and may buy time for a bottom-up resolution to emerge.

## Catalytic analysis

The objective here is to identify the forces contributing to the intensity of stakeholder outrage. They may be people or events, and they may provide a pathway for mitigation. In the Met's summer 2020 case, catalyzing forces included the murder of George Floyd in the United States and the unfavorable comments of some Black Met officers about stop and search. Those officers gave Dick a credible counterparty to work with in seeking longer-term solutions to the outrage.

Social media often channels catalyzing forces. It can provide anonymity, enabling otherwise circumspect individuals to express extreme views. Seeing such views encourages others to embrace, reinforce, and even sharpen them, a phenomenon known as *emotional contagion*. Social media algorithms also draw users deeper into outrage by shielding them from critical perspectives. Encouraging counterparties to tone down their social media engagement during discussions is therefore a good idea. (Again, rules of engagement should ideally be established before you apply them.)

## Step 3: Shaping and Bounding Your Responses

With some understanding of the drivers of outrage, managers can consider how to respond. Here they must strike a balance between not doing enough and doing too much. Considering the following two concepts can help.

### Asymmetric capabilities

In 2015 the food giant Nestlé faced a threat to its 100-plus-year presence in India when a routine test in a government food-safety lab found traces of monosodium glutamate (MSG) in its instant-noodles product Maggi, despite claims on the packaging that the noodles contained no added MSG. At first Nestlé ignored the issue, convinced that its practices were sound. Because about 75% of India's processed-food suppliers are small-scale domestic producers that routinely misstate their labels and have lower safety standards than Nestlé does, the company did not feel exposed to regulatory risk.

But later tests from other government labs indicated high levels of lead in Maggi noodles. The product, marketed as a health food and targeting children, came under further scrutiny. Nestlé then explained that although "no added MSG" was technically true, the product *did* contain naturally occurring glutamates. Regarding the lead content, Nestlé asserted that its own tests in India, Singapore, and Switzerland had confirmed the product's safety, and it conjectured that the later findings were a result of poor procedures at government labs. Its responses did not sit well with officials, some of whom issued regional recalls of Maggi noodles. The press piled on, and Nestlé's nearly 80% market share in instant noodles in India halved almost overnight, contributing to a 15% drop in stock price. Eventually, and at great cost, Nestlé withdrew and then relaunched the product without the label "no added MSG." (The lead concerns, it turned out, were indeed unfounded.)

The Swiss giant was expected to take responsibility for problems not of its own creation, even as more-culpable violators escaped, in large part because it had better *capabilities* than others to remedy the problem. In similar situations, therefore, managers need to consider four questions: (1) Are we directly responsible for the outrage? (2) Will our inaction exacerbate it? (3) Is acting to alleviate the outrage part of our (implicit) contract with stakeholders? (4) Do we want it to be?

Only if the answer to all four questions is no should you not act. For Nestlé the answer was no to the first, because it viewed the trouble as originating in regulatory inconsistencies. But its answers to the other three questions revealed that the company had good reason to act.

Take question two. Lead poisoning is very dangerous for children, and Nestlé's response left the matter unresolved. But ignoring looming serious harm to others invites outrage. Bioethicists' *rule of rescue* helps here: Our ethical instincts encourage us to aid those in imminent grave danger (regardless of culpability), even if we are held to a lower standard when the danger is less proximate. We are more impelled to help someone drowning in a pond than someone losing a livelihood to gradual flooding.

As for the third question, even in cases where the harm may be moderate and distant (as with the MSG issue), prior statements (describing Maggi noodles as a "health" product) may have set an organization up to address stakeholder concerns that it did not create.

For the fourth question, consider the advice offered by the Harvard professor Fritz Roethlisberger: When faced with a crisis, we often lament it as unfairly altering our otherwise well-drawn plans for the future. But what if that crisis is an opportunity to *actualize* those ambitions? Instead of complaining that a crisis is derailing you, treat it as an opportunity and lean in to your aspirations to shape your response. For Nestlé that could have meant using the Maggi crisis to affirm an inviolable commitment to safety.

Having determined an imperative to act, a company's next challenge is to ensure that it goes no further than necessary. Otherwise it may set unfulfillable expectations that can sidetrack the organization from its core mission or even bankrupt it. That brings us to the second concept.

## Shifting expectations

In 2012 the Swedish furniture behemoth IKEA was attacked in its own national media by an article revealing that it had airbrushed out images of women from direct-to-home catalogs circulated in Saudi Arabia. The company claimed that it was complying with Saudi laws and that the practice was long-standing.

The backlash in Sweden and IKEA's major markets in Western Europe, which accounted for 70% of sales, was swift. One Swedish minister commented, "For IKEA to remove an important part of Sweden's image and an important part of its values in a country that more than any other needs to know about IKEA's principles and values—that's completely wrong." The comment hit on an important truth: For years the company had branded itself as an extension of Swedish culture. A visit to the local IKEA, infused with Scandinavia-inspired kitsch, was like a trip to Sweden.

Over the years, IKEA had profited handsomely from that strategy, and it had mostly honored Swedish values: In the early 2000s, before ESG became fashionable, the company made commitments to fair labor and responsible environmental practices in its supply chain. As far back as the 1990s it had run commercials featuring same-sex couples. For a company that had long positioned itself as an exemplar of Scandinavian progressivism to be removing images of women from its Saudi catalogs was jarring.

IKEA entered Saudi Arabia in the early 1980s, shortly after the country's ruling family had thwarted a challenge to its power from radical Islamists. Having seen Iran's imperial family toppled for being too Western, the Saudi rulers chose to appear more hard-line. But 30 years later Saudi Arabia was a different place; in fact, even the Saudi media was bemused by IKEA's policy. Meanwhile, Scandinavian culture had become even more progressive. Expectations had shifted.

To avoid the adverse consequences of such shifts, an organization that makes a moral commitment, explicit or implicit, to its stakeholders must repeatedly ask itself three questions, which serve as a reality check for entities under pressure: (1) What is our strategy for authentically meeting this commitment? (2) What are the boundaries of this commitment, and how have they been communicated to stakeholders? (3) What is our strategy for dealing with shifting expectations around this commitment?

Through successive decisions involving its brand identity, IKEA had made a moral commitment to its stakeholders, in Sweden and in the rest of the West, to be a champion of Swedish values. The company had thought its commitment would be bounded by the laws of countries where it operated—but it had not effectively communicated that to its stakeholders. And IKEA was unprepared for the fact that as Swedish values became increasingly liberal, more would be expected of it.

Similar issues were at play in the London Met. Some stakeholders had argued that Dick's labeling the Met "institutionally racist" would powerfully signal its commitment to be part of the solution to racial injustice in society. The Met did not bear full responsibility for the outrage, but it had asymmetric capabilities for healing it. Nevertheless, Dick demurred. For the Met's own commissioner to accept the label would be politically seismic, and it would shift some stake-holders' expectations beyond her capacity to deliver. In addition, many within the Met considered the label demoralizing and offensive, and the commissioner could not afford mass exits or internal protests at a time of rising crime.

As that case shows, employee sentiment is a good way to evaluate possible responses to such quandaries. If trusted employees feel that you are not doing enough to address (external) stakeholders' outrage—or, conversely, fear that you might do too much—it is a good idea to rethink your approach. This, of course, underscores the value of giving your employees—who ideally are representative of other stakeholders—space to voice their perspectives.

Although the proportion of nonwhite officers at the Met had grown fivefold in the 20 years leading up to 2020, it still stood at only 15%—considerably lower than London's overall 40%. Until the Met became more representative of the community it sought to police, it would be unable to shake off the label "institutionally racist." So Dick made it a priority to rethink how the Met recruited and retained talent from the communities that trusted it least.

## Step 4: Understanding Your Power to Mobilize Others

After determining what you will do in response to the outrage, you must decide how to get it done. This is a two-stage process. First identify the sources—internal and external to the organization—of your ability to mobilize others: a spatial mapping of your power. Then ask how your power will evolve as you exercise it: a temporal mapping.

### Spatial mapping: where power comes from

It helps to divide power into four categories.

*Coercive power* is the ability to control others' actions through command. It may derive from your hierarchical authority and your ability to control scarce resources, such as by hiring, promoting, and firing individuals. It is the most basic source of managerial power, but it varies across types of organizations: Managers in nonmilitary public-sector bodies generally have less coercive power than do managers in private companies.

*Reciprocal power* is derived from exchanges. It can be purely transactional, as with a manager's power over an independent contractor in exchange for cash, but it does not have to be so. For example, no quid pro quo is necessarily expected in a social network, where power accrues from the *perception* of reciprocity. The greater your commitment to the exchange setting, the greater your power, because deep ties—forged over many years and interactions—are more likely to mobilize people.

*Emotive power* emanates from personal charisma. Like reciprocal power, it is based in relationships, but an exchange is rarely expected. Parents and children have emotive power over one another, as do people who share a deeply held faith.

*Rational power* is the ability to provide a reasoned (logical and evidentiary) explanation of your goals and methods. Managers often use it to bring well-informed peers on board.

To illustrate how spatial mapping can be helpful, consider the challenge confronting Meghana Pandit, the chief medical officer of Oxford University Hospitals (OUH), in 2020, early in the Covid pandemic, when scientists were uncertain about the virus and how to manage it.

The UK government had announced that elective surgeries should continue in OUH and other public hospitals. The goal was to prevent a huge backlog when the pandemic eased. Fearing shortages of personal protective equipment, some surgeons at OUH refused to comply, arguing that the order put their lives at risk. Pandit had to decide whether to enforce it and risk exacerbating an already emotionally fraught situation.

Although it is among the world's top hospitals, OUH had a checkered recent history. In 2018 it had reported eight "never events"—critical safety failures, such as wrong-site surgery, that should *never* happen. And staff surveys had shown that although many people took great pride in their own performance, teamwork was lacking, management was seen as not supporting staffers when mistakes were made, and the organization had a tendency toward both risk aversion and disregard of risk-management processes. The UK's Care Quality Commission had assessed OUH as "requiring improvement."

In early 2019 the OUH board appointed Pandit, who was then the chief medical officer at another hospital in Britain, to lead. Her focus through that year had been to reset the OUH culture toward patient safety and satisfaction, learning from mistakes, and trust in management. The initial results were promising, but the job was far from done when the pandemic hit and she was faced with the surgeons' resistance.

In that situation Pandit had considerable coercive power. She had final say over licenses to practice at OUH, so she could certainly enforce the government's order to continue with elective surgeries. She also enjoyed some rational power: As the surgeons' medical peer, she could speak with authority about the merits of the order as well as the Hippocratic ideal that the hospital was expected to achieve.

But Pandit lacked emotive power. As a woman and a member of an ethnic minority, she was outside the old boy network of Oxford physicians. They were unlikely to be swayed by her charisma. She also lacked reciprocal power of the transactional kind: As a public entity, OUH could not set salaries and bonuses; those were largely determined by national pay scales. And although Pandit was cultivating reciprocal power of the relational kind through the culture-change initiative, her efforts were only just beginning to take hold.

Despite her limited options, Pandit chose not to enforce the order, deferring to the surgeons in their moment of anxiety. The next stage of step four explains why.

## Temporal mapping: how power evolves

If Pandit had enforced the order, she would have risked eroding the small gains in reciprocal power she had recently earned and would most likely have made any further accrual impossible. Her cultural transformation depended on building staff members' trust in management; clamping down on their concerns at a time of great medical uncertainty would hardly help. In effect, Pandit was trading off short-run risks (invoking the government's ire and emboldening recalcitrant staffers) for a potential long-run win (a hospital with zero "never events").

She also wanted to preserve her coercive power for a time when she might truly need to use it. In March 2020 nobody had any sense of how long the pandemic would last, how severe it would be, and what kinds of command decisions it would necessitate. To expend that power so soon could prove very costly.

As you map the evolution of your power, consider the three basic ways in which it can be exercised: *implicitly*, through organizational culture; *indirectly*, through control of the agenda; and *explicitly*, through direct engagement (by yourself or by others acting for you). In general, the first approach is preferable to the other two, because effecting outcomes through shared beliefs can strengthen power, whereas the other options can erode it. But considering the feasibility of each way can guide you toward a decision.

If Pandit had been further along in her cultural transformation, the surgeons might not have even threatened revolt, because they would have trusted management to do right by them. But we cannot choose when crises will hit, and Pandit had to look for other approaches. The next obvious one was controlling the agenda. In March 2020 Pandit had many problems on her plate beyond the surgeons' concerns. They included setting up quarantined Covid wards, training medics to triage incoming patients for access to scarce ventilators and ICU beds, determining which hospital departments would have access to scarce protective equipment and Covid testing, crafting policies regarding staff leave to ensure a continually refreshed team on site to deal with the expected surge in patient volumes, and so on. By prioritizing those issues over the surgeons' anxiety, she could have implicitly conveyed a decision to them. But she feared that gaming the agenda in that way would undermine trust.

Instead she decided on direct engagement. But because she wanted to preserve her coercive power and had limited reciprocal power, she asked the surgeons for guidance on how to handle their situation. In effect she relinquished her coercive power to them, making them her agents. Her gamble paid off: Realizing from the perspective of power that their worries were but one ripple in a quickly swelling sea, the surgeons backed down. Roethlisberger's advice comes alive in Pandit's decision: She reached into a future version of OUH—one with a more trusting culture—to generate a solution to the present crisis.

## Step 5: Renewing Resilience

Admittedly, navigating the framework I have presented is demanding. Thus renewing resilience, organizationally and individually, is itself part of the framework. By "resilience" I mean the ability to recover from negative shocks. It includes, critically, a capacity for being intelligent about risks and associated failures.

### Organizational resilience

This comes from distributing decision-making responsibilities among trusted and competent delegates situated close to realities on the ground. It requires what economists call "relational contracts"— implicit understandings between managers and employees about the values that will guide each side's decisions and reactions to the decisions of others. Toyota offers a good example, specifically with its andon cord. Workers on the assembly line are encouraged to pull the cord if they notice a possible systemic manufacturing defect, stopping the entire process at great expense.

There are no explicit rules about when to pull the cord. If it were possible to specify any, then the cord would be unnecessary, and low-cost reliability would not be as elusive as it is. Instead, line workers and management have an implicit understanding that the former will not frivolously pull the cord and the latter will not punish the former if the cord is pulled (or not pulled) in error. Other car companies have tried for years to copy the Toyota system, but they have failed out of an inability to create the necessary relational contract.

An organization's resilience is also affected by how well its leaders manage the tension between dealing with today's problems and planning for better management of tomorrow's. From the long list of to-dos that Pandit had to consider alongside the possible surgeons' revolt, she chose cultural change as her foremost priority. But why focus on an intangible when so many tangibles needed attention?

The leadership expert Stephen Covey provides an answer: Managers often conflate the *urgent* with the *important*. There are always "urgent" issues on a manager's plate, especially in a crisis, and responding to them can very quickly become all-consuming. But the more leaders focus on firefighting, the less they focus on fire prevention—and the more fires they will need to put out in the future.

If Pandit had not prioritized cultural change in March 2020, she would never have had the capacity to address the stream of urgent decisions that came her way during a pandemic of indeterminate length. So she decided to continue building a culture of patient safety, confidence in management, and intelligent risk management—not to the exclusion of handling emergencies but with a view to ensuring that more of them could be handled by trusted and competent delegates.

### Personal resilience

This is perhaps the most elusive element in the framework. Managers are reluctant to talk about it because they fear that to do so will signal a lack of it. Here I have boiled down insights from various literatures into three takeaways.

**Do not conflate optimism with resilience.** A positive mindset is an element in individual resilience, but when managing in the age of outrage, it must be balanced with continual reappraisal of the situation at hand to allow for a recalibration of strategy and tactics. The author and consultant Jim Collins captured the difference when he suggested that leaders must have both an unfailing belief in ultimate victory and the daily discipline to acknowledge and address harsh realities.

**Beware learned helplessness.** We often create false narratives about adversity. Getting laid off from work is a traumatic experience that negatively affects self-worth. So someone who subsequently experiences another difficult work environment may attribute it to personal failings and struggle to address the challenges. Surmounting this learned helplessness involves acknowledging the false logic of our scripts, which usually requires external support through what experts call *active-constructive* relationships. Cressida Dick, for example, considers a community of trusted friends indispensable.

**Cultivate detachment.** According to the ancient Stoic philosopher Epictetus, "The chief task in life is simply this: to identify and separate matters so that I can say clearly to myself which are externals not under my control, and which have to do with the choices I actually control." I was drawn to this philosophy by some of the protagonists in my case studies, having noticed that managers who are successful in the age of outrage often manifest stoicism. The method is frequently misunderstood as advocating emotionlessness in the face of both pleasure and pain. For Stoics, however, the objective is not to deny emotions but, rather, to avoid pathological ones.

––––––––––––

Karl Popper, one of the 20th century's most influential philosophers, argued that science progresses by falsifying our theories about the world—a process of continual criticism. Ironically, he was also known for his "inability to accept criticism of any kind," in the words of Adam Gopnik. Observing this disconnect, Gopnik concluded, "It is not merely that we do not live up to our ideals but that we cannot, since our ideals are exactly the part of us that we do not instantly identify as just part of life."

I aspire every day to the framework offered here but do not always live up to it. I hope this admission comforts and encourages fellow managers who may be muddling through a polarized and uncertain world.

**Originally published in January–February 2023. Reprint** R2301G

# The Five Stages of DEI Maturity

*by Ella F. Washington*

SINCE THE MURDER OF George Floyd, in 2020, I've spoken with countless CEOs and chief human resources officers as they responded to the racial violence they witnessed that summer. And I've noticed a pattern: Leaders first tend to express deep concern and then ask if their company is instituting all the best diversity, equity, and inclusion (DEI) programs. They are eager to know what other companies are doing and how their own efforts stack up. Many firms take action because of something they see another company do—such as publicly declaring itself a champion of people of color or setting a top-down DEI strategy across the organization. But these grand stances usually fizzle out, leaving leaders throwing up their hands and saying, "DEI work is too hard. It takes too long to see results."

The fact is, DEI isn't a short-term project, and a company making big moves before it's ready will most likely fail to meet its objectives, leaving minority employees and community members continually marginalized. Moreover, doing so can give the organization a reputation for hollow, performative promises. Many companies that rushed to meet the moment in 2020, for example, pledged thousands of dollars to build racial equity but did not have a structure in place to support the implementation of new initiatives. As a result, they still haven't made any progress in improving their employees' and communities' lived experiences.

There is good news, however. More than 40 years of academic research and my experience helping hundreds of companies on their DEI journeys have shown me that companies tend to follow predictable stages on the DEI journey in sequence. When they understand which stage they're in, they can focus their energies on the right activities, making their DEI efforts more successful and making it more likely that they'll keep progressing.

In this article I describe the five stages: *aware, compliant, tactical, integrated,* and *sustainable.* For each one, I include questions for leadership teams to ask themselves to focus their efforts and keep moving forward. Although there's no one-size-fits-all DEI solution, a typical journey through these stages includes connecting top-down strategy and bottom-up initiatives around DEI, developing an organization-wide culture of inclusion, and, ultimately, creating equity in both policy and practice.

## Stage One: Aware

For many companies, the process of being intentional about DEI begins with a trigger—for example, a lawsuit, being called out by investors, or a traumatic experience such as George Floyd's murder. That gut punch of awareness can prompt soul-searching and a genuine desire to change course.

Companies entering the aware stage generally fall into one of two camps: successful older organizations that have never prioritized DEI or startups so deeply focused on survival that they've neglected to create strong human-capital practices. After a wake-up call, both camps often make high-minded public statements about their attitudes and intentions toward DEI. But what's really needed at this point is for them to be honest internally—especially within the leadership team. Leaders should ask themselves:

**Why does DEI matter to us personally?** Understanding colleagues' personal experiences of diversity or discrimination inside and outside the organization builds a necessary foundation of shared understanding and trust for further strategy work and for speaking with the broader organization about these topics.

# Idea in Brief

## The Problem

Companies looking to make progress on diversity, equity, and inclusion goals often make big declarations or try to implement ambitious top-down strategies before they have the right culture and structures in place. Such efforts often fail, leaving marginalized employees and customers no better off and giving companies a reputation for hollow promises.

## The Model

Academic research and the author's experience working with firms on DEI strategy suggest that companies typically move through five stages: aware, compliant, tactical, integrated, and sustainable.

## How to Use It

Knowing what stage your firm is in can help you decide where to focus your DEI energies most effectively and what questions your leadership team should be asking to keep you from getting stuck.

**Where do we want to go?** Setting a collective internal vision for the company's DEI work will help point you in the right direction as you get started. Leaders will have differing ideas of what DEI should look like, especially when they come from a broad range of backgrounds. So they must first agree on a vision of where to focus: Diversity of employees, having a better relationship with the community, building a more inclusive culture, and fixing the brand's reputation are all appropriate goals. Ultimately, companies should be doing *all* these things, but when they are just starting out, they need a specific target.

When setting goals, companies should take particular care to avoid benchmarking themselves against companies that may be at a later stage of DEI maturity. For example, the ice cream maker Ben & Jerry's, whose cofounders are the longtime social-justice activists Ben Cohen and Jerry Greenfield, boldly stated, "We must dismantle white supremacy" on its corporate web page and social media accounts in 2020. That is laudable, but if a company hasn't already built the structures and culture to act on such a stand—as Ben & Jerry's had—it will appear performative. Instead of making sweeping statements, companies in the aware stage should choose a narrower, more tactical goal.

Iora Health, whose mission is to "restore humanity to health care," is working to transform primary care. Since its founding in 2011, the Boston-based organization has opened 48 practices in 10 states and reduced hospitalizations of its patients by more than 40%. (It has since been acquired by One Medical, which Amazon recently announced plans to buy.)

In June 2020 Iora's cofounder Alexander Packard was shaken by the news of George Floyd's murder, and he knew that it was affecting his teams as well. He spoke candidly with four Black leaders in the organization, asking questions about race and racism, subjects he had never broached with them before. He was surprised to learn that many Black and Brown employees had never felt supported at the company. He had always assumed that Iora's mission—which led it to serve many people in marginalized groups—meant that it didn't need an intentional approach to DEI, but he realized that wasn't the case.

I led Iora's full leadership team in a two-part conversation about its DEI vision. During the first part, leaders spoke of their experiences with race. Some acknowledged that they had been largely unaware of issues of race and privilege; others shared deeply personal experiences from their childhood and professional life. The second part of the conversation built on the emotional momentum of the first. The leaders admitted that they weren't sure they were all aligned on the kind of diversity efforts they were looking for. They shared their own visions of what DEI should mean for the organization and then worked together to define what DEI would look like at Iora. They determined that for them, it meant serving a diverse patient population—including patients who might harbor racial biases—as well as supporting their Black and Brown team members. Navigating that tension has formed the basis of their DEI policies ever since.

## Stage Two: Compliant

Companies need to meet many industry and government requirements for diversity, such as EEOC laws in the United States. Additionally, businesses that have been subject to DEI lawsuits may have agreed to certain settlement terms. Some companies might pursue voluntary compliance and compare their DEI goals with those of competitors. At the compliant stage the thinking is typically, *We do DEI because we have to.* It's worth noting that a company could be compliant without ever going through the aware stage, but it would be ill-equipped to proceed any further without the foundational work done there.

Nearly a third of companies today find themselves in the compliant phase, according to a study of more than 10,000 knowledge workers in the United States, Australia, France, Germany, Japan, and

## A snapshot of companies' DEI progress

*A 2022 survey conducted in partnership with Slack's Future Forum asked more than 10,000 knowledge workers across six countries to evaluate their companies' DEI performance. Nearly a third of organizations are stuck in the compliant stage, the study revealed.*

**Which of the following statements best describes your company's approach to diversity, equity, and inclusion?**

| Aware | Compliant | Tactical | Integrated | Sustainable |
|---|---|---|---|---|
| 14.1% | 31.6 | 15.6 | 22.7 | 16.0 |
| DEI is new to my organization, and we are just becoming aware of its importance. | DEI in my organization is focused on compliance with EEOC and other legal requirements. | DEI has been connected to business initiatives and outcomes in pockets of the organization. | DEI is part of everything we do as an organization; we have both internal and external efforts on DEI. | DEI efforts are best in class and remain strong over time through our efforts to continuously improve and evolve. |

the United Kingdom (see the exhibit "A snapshot of companies' DEI progress"). This is partly good news: There is certainly a benefit to compliance. Regulations and requirements can spark meaningful changes in organizations because their terms and goals are so concrete. Whether it's talent selection, performance reviews, or diversity training and mentorship programs, companies are given specific direction on change. They often set up scorecards and use performance scores to determine leaders' bonus compensation. And doing the work to fulfill the specific terms of a compliance settlement can help an organization rebuild a reputation tarnished by poor DEI practices.

Still, it's notable—and concerning—that many companies become stuck in this stage. Just because a company is compliant doesn't mean its diversity initiatives are mature or connected with the organization's overall strategy. Many leaders of firms in this stage have not done the soul-searching needed to make real changes to their cultures. And although their diversity numbers may be good at the frontline level, employees from minority groups may still feel unsupported or unable to advance. Furthermore, research has shown that without an inclusive culture, a diverse workforce will not yield the tangible benefits of teamwork, creativity, better problem-solving, and so on. To go beyond the compliant phase, leaders should ask:

**Where can we set goals that are bigger than our compliance targets?** Companies that have managed to move past this stage have used the requirements imposed by regulations, not as end goals but as springboards for further efforts. For example, they push themselves to exceed their metrics for success or keep incentives in place long after regulatory requirements expire.

**How can DEI help us to meet our other goals?** Moving on from the compliant stage can be challenging because it requires the whole-hearted buy-in of senior executives and managers who may never have experienced the kinds of discrimination you're trying to fight. To get them on board, show them how DEI efforts can help your organization achieve its specific mission, values, and goals. While there is a risk that highlighting the business case for DEI obscures the ultimate ethical point that everyone should be treated with respect and have an opportunity to succeed, history has shown us the limits of moral conviction around DEI in the workplace.

In the 1990s the Denny's chain of fast-food restaurants was mired in numerous racial-bias lawsuits and scandals. After first contesting the suits, Denny's eventually settled with a large payout and a consent decree, which required the company to create written anti-discrimination policies, inform the public of those policies, provide training to all employees, and monitor and report any future incidents.

In 1994 Denny's hired April Kelly-Drummond to lead its diversity initiatives; under her guidance the company surpassed the terms of its consent decree. For example, the settlement mandated that all employees attend diversity training within 90 days of joining Denny's and attend a second session within 270 days; Denny's tightened those requirements to 75 days and 225 days. In fact, the company's strong performance led to its release from oversight by the Office of the Civil Rights Monitor a year early. After its release, Denny's didn't let up: It even placed a toll-free number in every restaurant to encourage others to help identify problems. The company also tackled bias in hiring beyond the scope of the original decree, broadened its recruitment efforts, and built a promotion pipeline. Further, it instituted an incentive structure around DEI goals. For example, 25% of senior management's incentive bonus was tied to the advancement of women and minorities.

In the 30 years since the lawsuits, Denny's has gone above and beyond the consent decree's original mandate, and its whole culture has changed. The chain has recaptured sales, repaired its reputation in local communities, and been named one of *Newsweek*'s best places to work.

## Stage Three: Tactical

Organizations in the tactical stage have moved beyond meeting the rules imposed on them and are fully engaged in executing their own DEI initiatives, which tend to be bottom-up. These companies might have flourishing grassroots efforts such as employee resource groups (ERGs) and teams that institute their own DEI processes—perhaps community guidelines for handling microaggressions or appointed devil's advocates in meetings to make sure diverse opinions are heard. There may be some top-down strategy or programming, such as a celebration of Pride Month, but it is largely executed independently by individual managers. Companies at the tactical stage are on their way to changing their cultures: Employees at all levels may engage in tough conversations about bias and give one another feedback; groups may take care to improve diversity of thought in their decision-making.

Yet companies in this stage typically still lack a strategic DEI approach that drives the entire business. Uncoordinated efforts mean that one area of the organization may champion DEI efforts while other areas ignore them. Consider Nike: Its 1988 "Just do it" campaign famously featured commercials for all customers regardless of age, gender, or physical fitness level, and the company publicly supported Colin Kaepernick in 2018 after his protests against racial inequality and police brutality. But Nike also has a troubling history of DEI offenses. In 2003 the company settled a racial-discrimination lawsuit filed by 400 employees, and in 2018 it faced a gender discrimination lawsuit alleging unequal pay for women and a hostile work environment. As we might expect with a company in the tactical stage, Nike's DEI efforts have been uneven, excelling in some customer-facing units but proving woefully inadequate in other areas. To better align their organizations, leaders should ask:

**What's our strategy?** You need to start defining an overarching DEI strategy that brings all your company's efforts together. Still, don't shoot too high: Companies that are most successful in implementing a new DEI strategy home in on a short list of priorities that can be connected to short- and long-term goals and metrics.

**Where do we need to standardize?** Do different units approach basic practices such as hiring differently? If some departments have made progress in creating an inclusive culture, learn from them and replicate their policies.

**How can we connect DEI work up and down the organization?** A feedback loop between team members, managers, and senior leaders is critical to the success of a DEI strategy. Executive buy-in can help clear cultural obstacles within a company and build a communal sense of responsibility for programs. Holding regular meetings between senior leaders and the leaders of grassroots efforts like ERGs can give you a good sense of whether your DEI efforts are improving corporate culture.

**What is our full sphere of influence?** Your company touches people beyond its employees: Take a close look at the impacts of discrimination or inequity across internal and external stakeholders, including employees, customers, partners, suppliers, shareholders, competitors, and your community. Look for ways to reduce existing inequities and build inclusion with those stakeholders as well.

The productivity-software firm Slack, which is in the tactical stage, has taken a decentralized and often employee-led approach to its DEI efforts. The company has encouraged employees to create an array of identity-based communities, and thus its DEI efforts are in large part the work of ERGs.

To ensure that these groups are more than social venues or places for commiseration, company leaders have made a concerted effort to regularly connect with them. Their monthly meetings uncover employee concerns and give ERGs early insight into the direction of the company and an opportunity to influence that path. ERGs also serve as a testing ground for new process ideas. ERG sponsors, meanwhile, are better able to understand the needs of employees and can give the groups greater exposure across the organization.

Slack has now begun to standardize some DEI processes. After the company created guidelines for interview questions to ensure that each candidate was treated similarly, regardless of the interviewer, the number of women in technical roles grew by almost 5% in a year. And Slack has brought its DEI gains to its larger sphere of influence with the introduction of Slack for Good, an initiative that aims to increase the number of people from historically underrepresented communities in the technology industry.

## Stage Four: Integrated

Once an organization has aligned internal and external efforts and connected top-down and bottom-up efforts, it has reached the integrated stage. An integrated organization has defined its DEI strategy, developed a culture of inclusion, and taken a close look at the impacts of discrimination and inequity across its internal and external stakeholders, seeking to address those challenges. Companies in this stage can truly say, "DEI is part of everything we do."

Despite this achievement, humility is the most common attribute of companies in this stage. For most, reaching this level has required experimentation to learn what works and what doesn't. Leaders of companies with long-standing and celebrated DEI programs must be modest enough to change course if what they are doing isn't working.

Leaders also worry that their success or even their efforts may be short-lived. DEI advances can often be linked to a particular event, to favorable market conditions, or to a particular leader's passion. To move on from the integrated stage, leaders must ask:

**What systems and structures do we need to create?** The current passion for and attention to DEI needs to be encoded in the way that the company works so that it persists beyond one leader's tenure or the current market cycle. The company needs to build programming that removes the burden of continuing the drumbeat for DEI from the shoulders of people in underrepresented communities themselves.

**Why not?** To move into the sustainable stage, companies must challenge the status quo and do things that simply weren't done before. They must also regularly evaluate the effectiveness of what they are doing for its impact on people and the business.

A common assumption I encounter in my work is that minority-owned businesses don't need to put as much effort into DEI. This assumption couldn't be more wrong, for many reasons. DEI goes beyond representation alone. Every organization, no matter its demographic makeup, must be intentional about the equitable nature of its systemic structures, such as hiring and promotion, and must focus on making the culture diverse, equitable, and inclusive.

Uncle Nearest is a whiskey distillery founded by Fawn Weaver, a Black woman who was inspired when she read the story of Nathan "Nearest" Green, an enslaved man in Tennessee who applied water-filtering techniques he had learned in West Africa to whiskey and became the first master distiller for Jack Daniels. Weaver launched a new distillery to honor his name; in a few short years it became the fastest-growing whiskey brand in the country and is now the best-selling African American–owned and African American–founded spirit brand of all time. Weaver built the company from the start with a clear DEI strategy, a goal to change her larger industry, a culture of confidence and self-expression, and a requirement for diversity in hiring.

But when Weaver tried to fulfill her vision for diverse recruitment, she couldn't find enough Black talent to hire. "One of the things I realized was that if I wasn't getting résumés of African Americans, then nobody in the industry was," she explains. "So the question became 'How do we get more African Americans interested in the spirit business? How can we be creative about building this longer-term pipeline?'" Weaver broke traditional hiring rules to achieve her goals: For example, she left positions open longer than her competitors did—up to two years—to maintain demographic diversity on her teams. Her willingness to challenge the status quo and think big has helped her to establish Uncle Nearest and ensure that its mission and commitment to DEI will outlive her tenure at the company. Uncle Nearest, founded in 2017, is still a new company, so it's hard to say it has reached the sustainable stage yet, but it is on its way.

## Stage Five: Sustainable

Organizations whose DEI efforts are deeply embedded in their corporate DNA have entered the sustainable stage. Their DEI efforts pass stress tests such as economic challenges and changes in leadership, and their leaders have a mindset of continuous improvement.

Take the technology giant Intel. In 2015 then-CEO Brian Krzanich announced a $300 million five-year plan to bring the company's workforce to "full representation" by 2020, initiating programs such as a $4,000 bonus for employees who successfully referred candidates from marginalized groups and a $5 million partnership to develop a high school computer-science curriculum for the Oakland Unified School District. In just six months the number of female and minority hires had surpassed the initial 40% goal for the year. Over the course of Krzanich's tenure hires from underrepresented communities increased by 31%, and Intel's female workforce increased by almost 43%.

But in 2018 Krzanich resigned after violating a nonfraternization policy with a colleague. Such a charged change in leadership could have meant an end to the policies championed by the outgoing leader. But Intel's next CEO, Robert (Bob) Swan, continued to set ambitious DEI goals. For example, in 2020 Intel pledged to increase the number of women in technical roles to 40% and to double the number of women and underrepresented minorities in senior roles by 2030. Swan left Intel in 2021, but that hasn't slowed Intel's commitment to DEI. According to its Corporate Sustainability Report 2021–2022, the company extended its Inclusive Leaders program and integrated the inclusion content into its Manager Academy training, which it began rolling out to its 13,000 managers. In 2021 it required all hiring managers to receive training in inclusive hiring practices. Further, it has initiatives in place to "increase the number of women hired for technician, engineering hardware and software roles" and has tied increased representation of women in technical roles to an annual performance bonus goal for all employees in 2022. DEI has become integral to its culture.

---

The work of DEI is never done. Without continued vigilance, even an organization that has designed systems and structures to remain sustainable through change can easily slide backward. True commitment to DEI requires continuous improvement by reassessing strategies and initiatives as the organization grows and as the world changes. For example, if you open your first-ever office in India, you will have new DEI challenges to solve. The same is true if some event in the world shines a bright light on inequity that you hadn't known was there.

Regardless of which stage you're in, knowing where you are on your DEI journey can help you focus on the right questions to keep moving forward.

**Originally published in November–December 2022. Reprint R2206F**

# To Avoid DEI Backlash, Focus on Changing Systems—Not People

*by Lily Zheng*

Perhaps in response to the critique that corporate efforts to achieve diversity, equity, and inclusion are all talk and no action, an increasing number of companies are taking the matter of diagnosing and resolving inequities more seriously. According to a recent survey, more than 40% either have already conducted a DEI survey or audit or are looking to do so "in the near future."

But in my own work as a DEI practitioner who often administers, analyzes, and helps companies act on these kinds of assessments, arriving at data-driven insights is only the tip of the iceberg. The far harder challenge is addressing organizational inequities without incurring *backlash*: strong adverse reactions from individuals and groups that undermine or compromise the positive outcomes DEI initiatives try to create.

Mandatory DEI training has been linked to *lower* levels of representation in leadership positions for Black, Latine, and Asian employees of all genders and white women, due to resistance from

existing leaders. Backlash is well-documented in response to organizational equity efforts like affirmative action policies, as well as
broader equity-related social movements. In what has since been
called the "#MeToo Backlash," a 2019 survey following up on the
impact of the #MeToo movement found that 19% of men were
*less* willing to hire attractive women, 21% were *less* willing to hire
women for jobs involving close interpersonal interactions, and 27%
now avoided one-on-one meetings with female colleagues.

It isn't only people from privileged groups that contribute to
backlash, either. When the "diversity" of candidates is mentioned
as a reason for their hiring, people rate the qualifications and skill
of a candidate from a marginalized group *lower*—even if they themselves are from that same group. And when marginalized employees are presented with a "business case for diversity," espousing
the benefits of diversity on business outcomes, they respond by
reporting a *lower* sense of belonging and less interest in joining the
organization.

Why is backlash such a large risk when DEI initiatives are put
into practice, especially when the vast majority of workers express
support for DEI in the abstract? Because people are strongly moti-
vated to protect their own sense of self-esteem, competence, and
"inherent goodness." When any of these things are challenged,
their gut reaction is to *resist* and *reject*. If people are told that their
language and interactions are biased, that constitutes a challenge
to their self-esteem. If people are told that "diversity" and not
"skill" played a role in their hiring, or that favoritism played a role
in their promotion, that constitutes a challenge to their sense of
competence. If people are criticized for being a member of a social
group that has negative associations, that constitutes a challenge
to inherent goodness. Regardless of how true any of these asser-
tions are, these framings run a high risk of resistance, rejection,
and backlash.

One powerful method to avoid backlash is by framing DEI initiatives to address inequities as changing systems, rather than changing individuals. By situating an organizational inequity in something

less "personal" than an individual or group, like a process, policy, or normalized set of practices, leaders can galvanize the workforce while lowering the risk that people feel personally targeted. Here are some examples of this approach in action, compared to framings that risk activating backlash.

*Backlash risk:* "Biased hiring managers are only bringing in candidates that look like themselves, which is why we have little racial or gender diversity. To address this, we should have all hiring managers go through training to address their biases."

*Systems framing:* "The hiring process doesn't have consistent guidelines or expectations, putting additional burden on hiring managers, creating an inconsistent experience for candidates, and making it difficult to connect our organizational strategy to our hiring strategy. To address this, we should create initiatives to support hiring managers, like implementing hiring panels, tracking the overall race and gender makeup of the candidate pool through each stage, and coming together to agree on how to make decisions fairly based on résumés and interviews."

*Backlash risk:* "Employees with disabilities and those who are neurodivergent aren't able to navigate the workplace as well as their nondisabled or neurotypical peers. To address this, we should give disabled and neurodivergent employees coaches and run a campaign to help all employees build empathy for these experiences."

*Systems framing:* "The employee experience is built around narrow assumptions about the 'ideal' employee that no longer hold true for our current workforce, which, among other things, is more disabled and neurodivergent than the workforce of the past. To address this, we should revisit employee onboarding, job design, and the manager–direct report experience to be more accessible, then integrate these changes into our general management training."

To put this approach into practice in your own organization, follow these five steps:

**1. Collect data to diagnose specific inequities in your organization**
Use a mix of quantitative and qualitative data, whether survey data, focus groups or interview data, network data, or HR data, with employee demographic data to identify inequities in specific aspects of the employee experience. Seek to understand not only "what" inequities exist, but also "why" and "how" they exist. Qualitative data can be a useful tool to assist.

**2. Communicate about initiatives using a systems-focused framing**
Make the case that the status quo is inequitable, pointing at the specific inequities you have identified, but maintain that the things to be "fixed" are specific systems, policies, processes, and practices, rather than the people engaging in them. Avoid blaming or shaming individuals or groups, and actively push back against fears that DEI initiatives will do so.

**3. As change-making efforts begin, appeal to "fairness"**
"Business case" rhetoric tends to alienate members of marginalized groups. "Multiculturalism" rhetoric that focuses largely on supporting marginalized groups may alienate members of advantaged groups. Instead, focus on "fairness" and stress that DEI efforts both require and will benefit members of all groups.

**4. Clearly lay out expectations for change alongside resources and support**
Communicate within the context of every initiative (for example, building a more inclusive shared language), the initiative's goals (fewer incidents of microaggressions and disrespectful language), and expectations for accountability (by the next yearly survey, an improved belonging score). Highlight primarily the support available to all (learning resources and leadership coaching), while underscoring the importance of achieving the initiative's goals within the expected timeline.

## 5. Sustain momentum by affirming effort and celebrating wins

Using DEI-related metrics, regularly identify and celebrate wins and achievements while praising the shared effort of all stakeholder groups. Ensure that these celebrations use a similar framing of fairness, universal benefit, and systems improvement as other steps in the process. Finally, regroup the organization around the next objective to meet, and repeat these steps as needed.

To genuinely address and resolve inequities, leaders must first understand the nuances and obstacles that so frequently stymie the initiatives they undertake. Backlash is no different, and what can appear at first glance to be knee-jerk defensiveness, ignorance, or fragility, under a more compassionate lens becomes our universal desire to be seen as dignified, competent, and inherently good. If leaders can protect these core needs while coming together to make change, they can create DEI initiatives that succeed.

**Originally published in September 2022. Reprint** H078QI

# The Essential Link Between ESG Targets and Financial Performance

*by Mark R. Kramer and Marc W. Pfitzer*

IN RECENT YEARS tremendous progress has been made in standardizing and quantifying measures of companies' performance on environmental, social, and governance (ESG) criteria. There has also been a surge in investor interest in companies that are rated highly on ESG performance or appear to be taking ESG goals seriously. Yet surprisingly few companies are making meaningful progress in delivering on their ESG commitments. Of the 2,000 global companies tracked by the World Benchmarking Alliance, most have no explicit sustainability goals, and among those that do, very few are on track to meet them. Even companies that are making progress are, in most cases, merely instituting slow and incremental changes without the fundamental strategic and operational shifts necessary to meet the Paris Agreement or the United Nations Sustainable Development Goals.

If companies neither integrate ESG factors into internal strategy and operational decisions nor communicate with investors about how improvements in ESG performance affect corporate earnings, then their claims about progress on sustainability goals are, at best, mere public relations—and at worst, deliberate misdirection.

A few companies—including Sweden-based homebuilder BoKlok; Enel, the Italy-based electric utility; South Africa–based insurer Discovery; Mars Wrigley, the candy and chewing gum division of Mars; and food giant Nestlé—are building sustainability into their strategy and operations by connecting financial and social performance. (Disclosure: These companies have been clients of our firm, FSG, or sponsors of its Shared Value Initiative.) This article offers a six-step process that other companies can use to fully integrate ESG performance into their core business models.

## The Problem with Separate Systems

Over more than 20 years of researching and working on sustainability issues with *Fortune* 100 companies around the world, we've found that when the measurement and accountability system for ESG performance is entirely divorced from the one that defines profitability and determines share price, leaders become blinded to the interdependence between the two types of performance. Indeed, the heightened attention to ESG reporting has not, for the most part, changed the way companies make decisions about strategy and capital investment. Nor has it helped reveal the tensions and opportunities that arise from understanding how ESG performance affects corporate profitability. As a result, most companies still treat sustainability as an afterthought—a matter of reputation, regulation, and reporting—rather than as an essential component of corporate strategy. Capital allocation and operational budgeting decisions continue to be made in ways that lead to social and environmental damage, while firms rely on meager corporate social responsibility budgets, philanthropy, and public relations to retroactively remedy or deflect the problems that those decisions create.

Consider ExxonMobil's announcement that it aims to become "consistent with" the Paris Agreement by reducing the environmental impact of its operations. At the same time, the company intends to continue to invest heavily in new oil and gas properties. Existing ESG rating systems allow the company to report on only the emissions from its internal operations, without taking into account the

## Idea in Brief

**The Problem**

Despite heightened attention to environmental, social, and governance (ESG) issues, surprisingly few companies are making meaningful progress in delivering on their commitments.

**The Root Cause**

Most companies are not integrating ESG factors into internal strategy and operational decisions and are providing investors with little to no explanation of how improvements in ESG performance affect corporate earnings.

**The Solution**

Identify the ESG issues material to your business. Factor in ESG effects when making strategic, financial, and operational decisions. Collaborate with stakeholders, redesign organizational roles, and communicate with investors about your new approach.

environmental consequences of the oil and gas it sells. By that flawed measure, ExxonMobil ranks in the top quartile out of nearly 30,000 companies in consensus ESG ratings. Its much-publicized commitment of $15 billion to low-carbon solutions ignores the $256 billion in 2019 revenues that were entirely dependent on fossil fuels, which makes the company the fifth-largest producer of greenhouse gases (GHG) on the planet. In short, neither ExxonMobil's massive impact on the planet nor the existential dilemma facing the company's economic future are fully reflected in the ESG rating or factored into management's strategic decisions.

Or consider Tyson Foods, a producer of chicken, beef, and pork. In 2016 Tyson made a commitment to reduce its greenhouse gas emissions by 30% by 2030, but since then, its GHG emissions actually increased an average of 3% annually. Our analysis suggests that it is impossible for Tyson to fulfill its financial projections and simultaneously meet its stated ESG goals. Tyson is not alone. Numerous companies have made ESG commitments that are incompatible with business realities—and as long as ESG metrics and financial reporting are disconnected, these inconsistencies will continue.

If companies are to move beyond mere posturing, leaders must confront the contradictions—and embrace the synergies—between profit and societal benefits and make the bold changes needed to actually deliver on the goals of the Paris Agreement and the United Nations' 17 Sustainable Development Goals.

Let's look at the six-step process for doing that in detail.

## 1. Identify the ESG Issues Material to Your Company

A good place to start is to consult the International Sustainability Standards Board's listing of material ESG issues by industry, defined as "those governance, sustainability, or societal factors likely to affect the financial condition or operating performance of businesses within a specific sector."

In some cases, the link between material ESG issues and financial performance is simple and direct. The bulk of ExxonMobil's revenues obviously comes from its customers' use of fossil fuels—even though it doesn't report on greenhouse gas emissions generated by customers in its sustainability report. The most material issue for Discovery, a global life and health insurance company, is customer health, which directly affects its financial performance. But unlike ExxonMobil, Discovery confronts the connection between those issues head-on. It uses a sophisticated set of rewards to encourage its subscribers (individuals and their dependents) to engage in healthier behaviors such as more exercise, better diets, and regular checkups. It tracks the cost of the incentives, their effectiveness in changing behavior, and the impact of behavior changes on medical costs and health outcomes.

Discovery uses this approach to continuously optimize the relationship between customer health and the company's bottom line. It has made numerous investments that differentiate it from other life and health insurers—such as giving its customers free Apple watches that enable the company to remotely monitor physical activity and track more than 11 million customer exercise readings per day. Promoting customer health as a core component of corporate strategy has created a unique competitive position and fueled Discovery's global expansion and superior profitability relative to other insurers. Rigorous academic studies by RAND, Johns Hopkins, and others have shown that the medical costs of Discovery's health insurance subscribers are 15% lower compared with those insured by local competitors, and the life expectancy of Discovery's life insurance customers is 10 years longer.

In other industries, the link between the social and environmental impact of a company's actions and profits may be more complex. In the food and beverage sector, the nutritional value of the products sold is an obvious and direct material issue; what's less visible are the operations of the suppliers of commodity inputs, which can represent 50% or more of all financial costs. Agricultural commodities like those Mars Wrigley uses are often sourced from smallholder farmers in South America, Africa, and Asia. While they offer a substantial cost advantage over commodities sourced from large-scale commercial growers in developed countries and generate income for smallholder farmers, the less sophisticated farming practices they use raise troubling social and environmental issues, including child labor, water scarcity, and deforestation, which accelerates climate change.

Mars Wrigley systematically tracks the carbon footprint and water intensity of the crops it purchases across the globe, along with farmers' income. Its challenge is to maintain a cost advantage by sourcing from lower-income countries while reducing poverty and environmental harm. Applying this approach to its sourcing of mint from smallholder farmers in India, for example, has resulted in a 26% increase in farmers' earnings and a 48% decrease in unsustainable water use, while allowing the company to sustain a significant cost advantage.

## 2. Focus on Your Strategy, Not on Reporting

The greatest social and environmental impacts of any company will be the result of fundamental strategic choices rather than incremental operational improvements. Startups, unencumbered by the past, often find strategic advantages by rethinking industry business models in light of current knowledge. When Discovery first entered the insurance market almost 30 years ago, it leveraged the ways that diet and behavior influence health to invent a more profitable business model that was unlike that of its more established health insurance competitors. In seeking to tap into consumers' concern about climate change, Tesla used new software and technology to invent the first popular electric vehicle. But many long-established companies still operate with business models that were developed decades—even centuries—ago, when leaders were unaware of or routinely ignored the impact that their businesses had on social conditions and the environment. They react to ESG issues only at the eleventh hour and are therefore poorly positioned to compete in a world where social and environmental impact drives shareholder value.

Virtually all incumbent automobile companies are now scrambling to catch up with the demand for electric vehicles after decades of focusing on incrementally improving the miles-per-gallon performance of their vehicles or reducing factory emissions. That is exactly the kind of strategic shift at the core of the business model that companies in every industry will need to make—and quickly.

The best way to ensure that your company is addressing its material social and environmental challenges is to relinquish your focus on modest change and improvements in reporting and, instead, identify and pursue bold new opportunities. Confront the fundamental question of how you will reinvent your business model and differentiate your company from competitors by building positive social and environmental outcomes into your strategy. Communicating a clear and compelling competitive strategy to create shared value—how you will pursue financial success in a way that also yields societal benefits—will carry far more weight with investors than marginal improvements in ESG metrics.

## 3. Optimize the Impact Intensity of Profits

Instead of relying only on conventional cost/benefit analyses and internal rate-of-return calculations to make budgetary and capital expenditure decisions, companies must begin to use equations that factor in the primary social and environmental effects of their operations. The "impact intensity of profits" is the relationship between a company's profits and its most important positive or negative effect on ESG issues. For the power company Enel, the primary issue is the environmental impact of its operational footprint, which means the company should make investment decisions that optimize profit per tons of $CO_2$ emitted. For Nestlé, the primary concerns are the nutritional value of its products and the ESG effects of sourcing from smallholders. The company might optimize profit generated per micrograms of nutritional value in its products and the cost of raw materials relative to farmer income and environmental impact in its sourcing. And for BoKlok, a joint venture between Skanska and IKEA, the primary societal benefit comes from expanding access to affordable and attractive housing in urban areas. Up to 40% of its developments are sold to social housing associations. This is the result of a decision-making framework that links profits to specific ceilings on the prices that the associations and other buyers have to pay.

Product design, product access, and operational footprint are three domains where companies must change their internal decision-making processes from focusing purely on financial returns to making a more sophisticated analysis that includes social and environmental consequences. The mathematical relationship between changes in environmental or social factors and the resulting changes in profit must become the guiding framework for decision-making at all levels within the company. The results are likely to lead to significantly different choices that not only improve ESG performance but also help reposition the company in ways that improve financial performance.

### Product design

Nestlé has long been concerned about the nutritional value of its food products, and until 2007, it made the same kinds of modest incremental changes in reducing salt, fat, and sugar content that other major food and beverage companies were making. But beginning in 2007, Nestlé began connecting the material issue of nutrition to its strategy and new-product design. This led the company to invest more than $1 billion annually in research to develop "nutraceuticals," nutritional supplements with measurable health benefits such as a reduction in postsurgical infections or a decrease in the number of seizures suffered by epileptics. These products, sold not through grocery stores but in pharmacies or administered in hospitals and reimbursed by insurers, have propelled the growth of Nestlé's nutrition and health science division. It is now the company's fastest-growing and most profitable division, with more than $14 billion in sales.

For Enel, whose main product is electricity, the shift toward a low-carbon world has created new product opportunities. Enel now offers power-management services to its customers: It helps homeowners reduce electricity usage, works with businesses to optimize the operations of fleets of electric vehicles, and guides cities in building infrastructure in ways that continuously minimize power consumption and provide charging options for electric vehicles.

Companies that don't link the social and environmental consequences of their businesses directly to their business models and strategic choices will never fully deliver on their ESG commitments. Tyson Foods will continue to expand sales of beef as the main driver of profits to meet its financial targets even though beef generates the largest amount of greenhouse gas emissions per ton of protein of all the company's products. If Tyson were serious about optimizing profits and substantially reducing GHG emissions, it would need to make a dramatic shift in strategy and invest much more heavily in plant-based and cellular meat alternatives—a strategy that would dramatically reduce its emissions and potentially increase its profit per ton of protein produced as the plant-based-meat segment scales and matures.

### Product access

The objective of BoKlok is to profitably develop energy-efficient housing that teachers, nurses, and other lower-wage workers can afford to buy or rent. BoKlok uses a detailed analysis of people's salaries, cost of living, and typical monthly expenses as the benchmark for ceilings on its sale prices. Manufacturing the homes in a factory reduces both the cost of the housing and the carbon emissions produced during construction. (BoKlok has made a commitment to reach net-zero carbon emissions—from manufacturing, sourcing, and even the energy consumption of the homes it builds—by 2030.) Factoring access and affordability into its investment decisions has heavily influenced its choices—such as collaborating with municipalities in Sweden, Finland, Norway, and the United Kingdom to buy land. The reward is a rapidly expanding new market opportunity: Since creating its industrialized affordable-housing model in 2010, BoKlok has built 14,000 homes, while routinely outperforming Skanska's conventional construction business on a return-on-capital-employed basis.

## Operational footprint

Greenhouse gas emissions from electricity generation is Enel's most material issue, along with its customers' energy use. So Enel has invested €48 billion over three years (2021 through 2023) in renewable power generation, upgrades to improve the efficiency of its distribution network, and new energy-saving technologies for end users. These investments will help Enel reduce its reliance on coal-fired power plants from 10% in 2021 to only 1% by 2023. They will also dramatically increase profit per ton of $CO_2$ emitted and decrease emissions from 214 grams of $CO_2$ to 148 grams $CO_2$ per kWh—while delivering an EBITDA compound annual growth rate of 5% to 6% to shareholders.

A primary issue for Mars Wrigley, as noted above, is the footprint of its commodities sourcing. So the company systematically sets baseline performance measures for climate, water, land, gender-specific income, and human rights across each of its commodities. Each commodity has a different footprint: For cocoa the most critical ESG factors are farmer poverty and deforestation; for dairy products, land and water use are important. Issues vary even within a given commodity: Sugar is a key ingredient in Mars Wrigley's products, but if it is sourced from beets, the biggest consideration is water use, whereas sourcing from sugarcane raises issues of poverty and human rights.

If Mars Wrigley had ignored suppliers' social and environmental factors, the drive to maximize profit would inevitably have led it to purchase from smallholders with the worst social and environmental impacts, given that labor and environmental practices tend to improve with more sophisticated and costly farming. Buying higher-priced commodities from large-scale commercial farmers might improve the company's ESG performance, but doing so would also increase its costs and do nothing to reduce the poverty of smallholders and the environmental degradation that their farming practices cause. Integrating sustainability factors into its procurement process has enabled Mars Wrigley to maintain a cost advantage and, by making carefully calibrated investments in helping small farmers, communities, and supply chain partners change their practices, to reduce poverty and harm to the environment.

## 4. Collaborate to Avoid Trade-Offs Between Profit and Societal Benefit

Win-win solutions that improve both societal benefits and profits are easy to adopt, but most companies stop short when they confront trade-offs that require sacrificing profit for improved social or environmental performance. Such trade-offs, however, often can be avoided by collaborating with other stakeholders. In fact, many levers that affect a company's impact intensity of profit are controlled by only a few external stakeholders.

Sugarcane cutters in Latin America have, for decades, been paid in cash on the basis of the weight of the sugarcane they cut. The pace at which cutters work determines how much distance they cover in a day, but the weight of the cane they cut depends on factors outside their control, such as the type of sugarcane planted, the irrigation and fertilization practices, and the weather. The team leaders, who traditionally hand out the cutters' pay, have complete discretion in how much to pay each worker, and there are no controls to ensure that each worker receives their due. The result is that many cutters take home far less than a living wage. An ongoing pilot project involving sugarcane mills, purchasers, and local NGOs has found a way to address these issues: It combines a minimum daily wage with additional compensation based on the amount cut. Digital payments are transferred directly to the cutters' mobile phones to ensure that they promptly receive what they have earned. Together these measures can raise cutters' wages by 25% while increasing the cost of sugarcane to the mills by less than 5%, most of which is expected to be offset over time through productivity gains.

Enel found success with a different type of collaboration. The company needed world-class engineering talent in order to make its shift from fossil fuel to renewable energy, but the most talented environmental engineers did not want to work for an electric utility that still relied heavily on fossil fuel. So the company turned to crowdsourcing. It has posted more than 170 of its most difficult technical problems on its Open Innovability digital platform, which reaches 500,000 "active solvers" from more than 100 countries. So far, they have proposed some 7,000 solutions to those challenges. Enel's engineers evaluate them and either award cash prizes to winners or establish joint ventures with them.

For example, the shift to renewable power depends, in part, on batteries large enough to smooth out the fluctuations in solar- and wind-generated power for an entire city. This is a big challenge because the storage capacity of today's batteries is severely limited and extremely expensive. As electric vehicles become more common, electric car batteries could be used to store power and provide it when needed. Using just 5% of the stored energy in car batteries could balance the power grid for an entire city. Enel had the idea but lacked the software needed to allow the batteries to contribute electricity to the grid. A six-person startup based in Delaware learned of the opportunity through the Open Innovability platform and provided the software solution.

Collaboration with other stakeholders, whether companies, governments, or NGOs, requires a new degree of cross-sector trust and collaboration. The game of blaming one another for social or environmental problems will have to give way to a partnership in which everyone endorses a shared agenda. In the process, positive outcomes become compatible with profits, and baseline measures, strategies, and investments are developed jointly.

## 5. Redesign Organizational Roles

Despite the increased attention to ESG performance, most companies have done little to change their organizational roles and structures to integrate sustainability into operations. CSR departments are typically very small and uninvolved in strategic and operational decisions. They focus primarily on stakeholder and government relations, philanthropy, and ESG reporting. But if ESG criteria are to be integrated into key decisions, then people with sustainability expertise need to be at the table when strategic and operational decisions are made.

Enel has made that change. Its innovation and sustainability functions are combined under a "chief innovability officer," who oversees, on a matrix basis, a team of people who hail from every department to ensure that all decisions include a sustainability analysis. Mars Wrigley created the combined role of "chief procurement and sustainability officer." BoKlok and Skanska similarly created an executive vice president position to oversee sustainability and innovation.

Incentives must also be aligned. Compensation schemes must reward performance for reaching not just financial but also social and environmental goals. Some ESG-related compensation bonuses are "artfully" designed so that they can be awarded even if emissions increase or environmental damage worsens. Obviously, that renders such incentives ineffective. Companies that take ESG goals seriously make sure that a significant part of executives' bonuses are dependent on achieving them. At Mars, the top 300 corporate leaders receive long-term incentive compensation (above salary and annual bonuses) on the basis of their success in achieving equally weighted financial and emissions-reduction goals over a three-year period. And Mastercard recently announced incentive compensation for all employees that includes performance metrics around three material issues: carbon emissions, financial inclusion, and gender equity.

## 6. Bring Investors Along

Companies must explain to investors their strategies for improving the impact intensity of their profits, communicate their commitments to achieving explicit goals, and report publicly on their progress.

Spelling out how the company is incorporating positive social impact into its business model will carry far more weight with investors that care about climate targets and sustainable development goals than flawed and inconsistent ESG rankings.

Nestlé, for example, which has been steadily reducing sugar, salt, and fat across its product portfolio for more than a decade, began only in 2018 to disclose to investors that these healthier foods had faster growth rates and higher profit margins than traditional offerings. Enel has long described its shift to renewables in its sustainability reports and taken pride in its efforts to advance the UN's Sustainable Development Goals, but only in November 2019 did it first highlight the financial value driven by the renewables business model in its Enel Capital Markets Day investor presentation. In the following three months, when most stocks plunged because of the Covid-19 pandemic, Enel's share price increased almost 24%, a change that management attributes to this shift in communication strategy. Unless companies clearly explain the financial benefit of their ESG improvements to their investors, they will not see the value of those efforts reflected in their share prices.

---

We cannot continue the path we are on today, where companies' social and environmental actions are after-the-fact interventions disconnected from strategy and decision-making. Focusing on shared value and the economics of impact will lead companies to make fundamental changes to their business models, capital investments, and operations, generating meaningful opportunities for differentiation and competitive advantage. In doing so, they will create an economy that truly works to close social inequities and restore natural ecosystems.

**Originally published in September–October 2022. Reprint** R2205K

# Make the Most of Your One-on-One Meetings

*by Steven G. Rogelberg*

**TURNOVER WAS HIGH** on Bill's team—higher, in fact, than on most other teams at his company. Although Bill thought of himself as a good manager, exit interviews with his departing team members suggested that they hadn't felt meaningfully engaged or fully supported in their roles and had tended to step on one another's toes with their assignments.

What, exactly, was Bill doing wrong? One area stood out when I spoke with him and his team: He held fewer regular one-on-one (1:1) meetings with his direct reports than his peers at the company did. When he did meet with team members individually, the subject tended to be a critical issue he needed help with rather than their work or their development.

Bill, a composite of managers I've worked with and studied, clearly had a blind spot when it came to 1:1s. Such blind spots are not uncommon. Of 250 direct reports I surveyed recently, nearly half rated their 1:1 experiences as suboptimal. That's hardly surprising, given that few organizations provide strong guidance or training for managers about when and how to meet individually with their employees. But my research shows that managers who don't invest in such conversations—who view them as a burden, hold them too infrequently, or manage them poorly—risk leaving their team members disconnected, both functionally and emotionally.

The best managers recognize that 1:1s are not an add-on to their role—they are foundational to it. Those who fully embrace these meetings as the place where leadership happens can make their teams' day-to-day output better and more efficient, build trust and psychological safety, and improve employees' experiences, motivation, and engagement. The managers thrive in turn, because their success is tied to the performance of those reporting to them.

I've been studying teams, leadership, engagement, and meetings at work for decades, and in the past three years I've set out specifically to learn what makes 1:1s work best by doing three studies: a global survey of 1,000 knowledge workers, a U.S. survey of 250 people who either lead or participate in 1:1s, and interviews with nearly 50 top leaders at various *Fortune* 100 companies. I've discovered that although no one-size-fits-all approach exists, there are some useful guidelines for managers. Most important is that the manager should consider the meeting a focused space for the direct report and make that explicit. The meeting should be dominated by topics relating to the needs, concerns, and hopes of the employee, who should take an active role in presenting them. As the manager, your responsibilities are to ensure that the meetings occur, actively facilitate them, encourage genuine conversation, ask good questions, offer support, and help each team member get what's needed for optimal short-term performance and long-term growth.

In this article I'll lay out how to prepare for and facilitate effective 1:1s.

## Before the Meetings

Setting up your 1:1s should entail more than dropping invites onto your team members' calendars. You should lay the groundwork for your conversations and plan the logistics to best fit each report's unique needs.

### Communicate the initiative or your reboot of the initiative

Whether or not the practice of holding 1:1s is new to your team, announce it at a team meeting so that everyone gets the message at

## Idea in Brief

Few organizations provide strong guidance or training for managers on meeting individually with their employees, but research shows that managers who don't hold these meetings frequently enough or who manage them poorly risk leaving their team members disconnected, both functionally and emotionally. When the meetings are done well, they can make a team's day-to-day activities better and more efficient, build trust and psychological safety, and improve employees' experience, motivation, and engagement at work.

Although there's no one-size-fits-all approach to one-on-ones, they are most successful when the meeting is dominated by topics of importance to the direct report rather than issues that are top of mind for the manager. Managers should focus on making sure the meetings take place, creating space for genuine conversation, asking good questions, offering support, and helping team members get what they need to thrive in both their short-term performance and their long-term growth.

the same time and no one feels singled out. Tie the meetings to your organization's values (such as the importance of hearing employees' voices) and to your personal values (such as striving to be a supportive leader). Also stress that these conversations are not meant to signal dissatisfaction with your team's work and are not about micromanaging; rather, they are opportunities for you and each member to get to know each other better, learn about challenges, and discuss careers, and for you to give help when it's needed. This is also a good moment to tell your team members what you need from them to make the meetings successful: They should drive the agenda with key priorities, be curious, be actively engaged, communicate candidly, think deeply about problems and solutions, and be willing to ask for help and act on feedback.

### Determine cadence

My research suggests that you should adopt one of three plans for the frequency of 1:1s:

1. You meet with each of your team members *once a week* for 30 minutes or so. In my surveys, employees, regardless of job

level, rated this approach the most desirable; it also correlated with the highest levels of engagement.

2. In the second-highest-rated plan you meet *every other week* for 45 to 60 minutes.

3. In a *hybrid* plan you meet with some team members weekly and others every two weeks.

Whichever plan you choose, aim to spend roughly equivalent amounts of time with employees over the course of a month so that all team members get the same in-person support from you. To determine the right cadence, consider:

- *Team member experience.* Weekly meetings are ideal for more-junior employees and those who are new to the team. They allow you to provide coaching and other support for the employees' growth and development and to build a relationship.

- *Manager tenure.* Similarly, if *you* are new to the team, weekly meetings are ideal for establishing relationships and alignment.

- *Team size.* If your team is large (10 or more), consider holding 1:1s every other week so that you can stagger them across a longer time span. You may need to reduce the time allotted to each meeting. To ease the load associated with a large team, some managers introduce peer mentoring, in which team members give guidance and feedback to one another rather than rely solely on the manager.

- *Remote or in person.* If your team is remote, weekly meetings can help counter a lack of spontaneous face-to-face contact.

- *Team member preference.* Finally, give your employees a voice in the decision.

I've seen some managers, mostly senior leaders, opt for three or four weeks between 1:1s, but investing only 60 minutes or so with each team member every month makes building a trusting relationship difficult. And because more-recent events are easier to recall, the longer time lapse also means that you're less likely to discuss any issues that arose several weeks prior to the meeting. These meetings are most effective when you can build momentum around specific areas of the direct report's activities and growth. A monthly cadence makes that more challenging. But if your team members are seasoned and have worked with you a long time, and you are readily available for impromptu conversations, this cadence can work and is preferable to nothing. However, employees rated this option as least desirable, and it was associated with smaller gains in engagement.

Finally, avoid canceling 1:1s, which can hamper your team members' progress and make them feel that they are low on your priority list. This was one of Bill's problems: He readily canceled these meetings if he got busy. That sometimes demoralized his team members; they also found themselves duplicating efforts or working at cross-purposes because they hadn't had a chance to coordinate their work through Bill. If you must cancel, reschedule the meeting right away, ideally for the same week—even if that means moving the meeting up rather than moving it out. Another option is to reduce the length of the meeting: Some time together is better than none at all.

### Set a location

In my research, employees rated virtual 1:1s as slightly less desirable than those held in person, but they rated the ultimate value of the meetings similarly regardless of which form they'd taken. If you can meet in person, choose a location where you and your employee will feel at ease, present, and free of distractions. In my surveys the most highly rated location was the manager's office or a conference room; the lowest was the direct report's office. Support for outside locations, such as coffee shops, or taking a walk near the office, was uneven, so don't assume that everyone would welcome them. Talk to your team members in advance to gauge where they feel most comfortable.

### Create an agenda

Many managers assume that 1:1s are too informal to require an agenda, but my research shows that having one is a strong predictor of the effectiveness of the meeting, whether it was created in advance (which is ideal) or at the meeting itself (if necessary).

Even more critical, though, is the employee's involvement in the agenda's creation: Both direct reports and managers rated meetings most highly when the reports contributed to or established the agenda themselves. Bill's habit of organizing his 1:1s around his own priorities and needs meant that his team members' concerns were usually relegated to the end of the meeting—and often went unaddressed if time ran out.

Collaborating on an agenda can be as simple as having each party create a list of topics to discuss. In the meeting the two should work through first the employee's list and then the manager's, as time allows. (Both should review their notes from previous 1:1s while preparing their lists in case some topic requires follow-up.)

Alternatively, some managers create the agenda from broad questions, such as: What would you like to talk about today? How are things going with you and your team? What are your current priorities, and are there any problems or concerns you would like to talk through? Is there anything I can help you with or anywhere I can better support you? What do I need to know about or understand from your perspective?

A warning: Both these approaches tend to prioritize immediate tactical issues and fires to be put out. However you plan your agendas, periodically weave in longer-horizon topics such as career planning and developmental opportunities—by either taking five or 10 minutes at every meeting to discuss those areas or dedicating one out of every three or four meetings to addressing them. (See the exhibit "Sample questions for 1:1s" to get a sense of issues that should be discussed over time.)

## At the Meetings

Once you've prepared for a meeting, a fruitful discussion will depend on your ability to create a setting in which your employee feels comfortable. A valuable 1:1 addresses both the practical needs and the personal needs—to feel respected, heard, valued, trusted, and included—of the employee. To ensure that a meeting does so:

## Sample questions for 1:1s

**Work style preferences**
- Tell me about the best manager you've ever had. What did that person do that you thought was most effective and helpful?

**Well-being and engagement**
- What is your favorite part of the job?
- Least favorite?

**Roadblocks, obstacles, or concerns**
- Is anything slowing you down or blocking you right now?
- How can I help or support you?

**Culture and team dynamics**
- What aspects of our team culture do you think we should maintain, change, or work on?

**Asking for input**
- What feedback from me could be helpful—any particular projects, tasks, skills?
- Would you like more or less coaching or direction from me?

**Career development and growth**
- What would you like to be doing in five years?
- What work are you doing here that is most in line with your long-term goals?

**Personal connections**
- What are your favorite podcasts, books, or hobbies?

## Set the tone

First, be present. Turn off email alerts, put your phone away, and silence text notifications. Remind yourself as the meeting begins that it is fundamentally about your employee's needs, performance, and engagement.

As you go into the meeting, check your emotional state. Research shows that the mood you bring to a meeting has a contagion effect, so start out with energy and optimism. Reiterate your goals and hopes for the meeting and then move to some non-work-related topics, rapport building, wins, or appreciation to generate momentum and foster feelings of psychological safety. One problem for Bill was that he viewed 1:1s as merely another task on his already long list—something to just get done. That affected how he facilitated (or failed to facilitate), how he listened, how he collaborated, and how he engaged.

### Listen more than you talk

The biggest predictor of a 1:1's success, according to my research, is the employee's active participation as measured by the amount of time that person talks during the meeting. The ideal is anywhere from 50% to 90%. The agenda will have some influence on that, but you as the manager should carefully avoid talking more than your employee does.

In addition, listen actively to fully understand your direct report before you speak yourself. Display genuine interest without judgment and acknowledge the employee's viewpoint even if you disagree with it. Ask questions that clarify and constructively challenge that viewpoint. Encourage your team member to provide thoughts on the matters at hand and potential solutions to problems. Stay vigilant about your body language and reactions to ensure that you're creating a welcoming and safe space.

### Add your perspective

Once you've listened closely, there will be moments in the meeting when you need to contribute your point of view. A 1:1 provides an excellent opportunity for you to give honest and specific feedback on your direct report's perspectives or actions. It is also a good place for you to engage in collaborative problem-solving by truly understanding whatever issue is at hand, pooling information, identifying root causes, and creating a solution that both parties feel good about. If the team member's solution is viable—even if it's not better than your own—it's important that you go with it. That sends a strong message and creates more commitment to the team member's proposed path forward.

### Be flexible

As you work through your established agenda, allow the conversation to move organically as needed to provide value. Focus on the items that are most critical. If some items go unaddressed, move them to the following 1:1. Let your employee know at the outset that real-time changes can be made to the agenda if a critical item emerges.

Also, to best connect with each direct report, consider that person's preferences regarding communication, collaboration, and so forth, and adjust your leadership approach accordingly. That will increase engagement and inclusion, deepen the relationship, and create trust.

### End well

Clarify takeaways and action items for both parties, including how you will support next steps. When both the manager and the employee document these, chances are better that the actions will be carried out. It also builds continuity between meetings and allows for needed follow-up. After Bill implemented this change, he was reminded that his 1:1s were not mere transactions to get through but, rather, represented employees' evolving stories—something to be nurtured and developed over time. Finally, show gratitude and appreciation for your direct report's time—and start and stop on schedule to demonstrate those feelings.

### Improve over Time

Ideally, both parties should leave the conversation feeling valued, respected, and well-informed, with clarity about next steps on projects, solutions to problems, and the commitments that each of them has made. However, the most important metric for success is whether your employee found the meeting both valuable tactically and fulfilling personally.

To learn where you stand and to improve these meetings over time, start by asking each team member for feedback and ideas to make future 1:1s better. Or you can anonymously survey your team with three basic questions: What's going well with the 1:1s? What's not going well? Do you have ideas for improving them? Know that what works at one time for your 1:1s may not work at another time, and what is comfortable for one direct report may not be so for another. So even if you think your current pattern is successful, keep trying new things.

What Bill learned from his first survey about 1:1s was sobering. Even more than in the exit interviews, team members raised concerns about whether he really cared about their performance or growth, citing his frequent cancellation of meetings and saying that they often couldn't get a word in edgewise. But once Bill had taken their feedback to heart, the atmosphere on his team began to shift. As he committed to meeting regularly with his employees on topics of importance to them, he found that they seemed more committed to—and proficient at—their work.

———————

Regular individual meetings with each of your team members may feel like a burden. But meeting for 30 minutes each week with one person adds up to no more than 25 hours over the course of a year. That's not too high a price to pay to bolster your team's and your company's performance; support retention and prevent you from spending just as much time (or more) recruiting and onboarding re-placements; and help each of your team members grow and achieve.

**Originally published in November–December 2022. Reprint R2206L**

———————

# Five Questions Every Manager Needs to Ask Their Direct Reports

*by Susan Peppercorn*

Sara, a departing employee, sat across from her company's HR leader for an exit interview. As a marketing executive for a financial services company, she was resigning after five years to take a CMO role at a fintech startup.

When the HR director asked Sara, "Is there anything else we could have done to keep you here?" Sara paused. "Yes. I wish there had been conversations about my career goals and opportunities for growth," she said.

This is just one of the discussions that often takes place too late, after top talent is already on the way out the door.

As the number of workers quitting their jobs continues to swell amid the Great Resignation, soon-to-be-former employees are finding themselves in exit interviews with HR representatives who hope to gain a clearer sense of what's happening inside the company—and who often learn, after the fact, things that management was unaware of. Exit interviews provide "a way to find out what is happening, or what has happened, that may be motivating this employee . . . to leave," according to Yuletta Pringle, knowledge adviser at the Society for Human Resources Management.

Yet as the previous dialogue illustrates, these conversations may be too little too late. In a recent Gallup study, more than half of employees surveyed said that no one—including their manager—had talked to them about how they were feeling in their role in their last three months before they quit. And 52% of exiting employees stressed that their manager or organization could have done something to prevent them from leaving their job.

Having coached hundreds of employees in career transition for more than a decade, I can validate these findings. Countless clients have told me they wished their employer had asked them questions to encourage their growth *before* they resigned. They wanted these questions to come from their manager proactively, rather than retroactively from HR.

Before asking questions as a manager, though, it's critical to know what motivates employees to stay with an organization and why. Gallup research shows 12 needs that managers can meet to improve employee engagement, including:

- Prioritizing employee development
- Facilitating a sense of purpose
- Caring about employees
- Considering employee opinions
- Focusing on employee strengths

These five measures map closely with research recently published by *Harvard Business Review* on strategies to boost retention. With these five needs in mind, consider incorporating the following questions into routine check-ins with your direct reports so that you can ask employees the questions they want to hear before they're gone.

### How would you like to grow within this organization?
Career development is the most critical of the elements identified by Gallup, and two-thirds of people—regardless of their level—leave their company because of a lack of career-development opportunities. With this in mind, it's important to figure out what growth opportunities each employee needs for optimum development, whether through sponsorship, coaching, mentoring, visibility, or challenging work assignments.

To get at the answer, you might also ask, "What role would you love to have (whether it exists or not), and what can I do as your manager to encourage your development in this company?"

### Do you feel a sense of purpose in your job?
In the five years that Sara worked for the financial services company that she was resigning from, she never felt that her work impacted people's lives in a meaningful way. By joining a fintech company committed to improving the accessibility and affordability of financial services for underserved populations, she was excited that her marketing efforts could make a difference in the lives of people who needed access to capital. Her employer and manager missed an opportunity to tap into Sara's sense of passion and purpose in her marketing role.

Managers can play a meaningful role in helping employees understand how their roles contribute to the organization's broader mission. But helping employees feel a sense of purpose must go deeper than this to tap into what's purposeful to employees about their job and connects with their own values.

### What do you need from me to do your best work?
The most effective managers respect and care about their employees by knowing them as individuals, acknowledging their achievements, having performance conversations, and conducting formal

reviews. These supportive behaviors build a work environment where employees feel safe experimenting with new ideas, sharing information, exploring development opportunities, and supporting each other.

As you explore what your employees need to do their best work, you might also ask, "What is your biggest frustration, and what action can I take to help you deal with it? What have you been trying to tell me that I've not been hearing? How would you like to be recognized?"

### What are we currently not doing as a company that you feel we should do?

The best managers let workers know that their opinions count by promoting open dialogue and providing honest feedback on employees' opinions and suggestions, supporting good ideas and addressing unfeasible ones. By asking individual team members what they feel the company could be doing better, what market opportunities the organization might be overlooking, and how to leverage company resources more effectively, you're validating that their thoughts matter.

You might also ask things like, "Are you satisfied with our current work-from-home or hybrid policy? If not, what do you think needs to change? How satisfied are you with the tools you use to communicate with your colleagues when working remotely?"

### Do you have the opportunity to do what you do best every day?

When Sara was in her marketing role, her concentration was on data analytics. Although she learned how to master analyzing customer-use data, she never considered it one of her strengths. Her new role will allow her to concentrate on branding and audience acquisition, areas that she enjoys and excels in. Once again, her former employer missed an opportunity to harness the best of Sara's talents before she took them to a new organization.

To determine whether your employees are focusing on their strengths, you might also ask, "What is the best part of your job? Which of your talents are you not using in your current role? What part of your job would you eliminate if you could?"

When managers make checking in with these five questions a regular part of how they interact with their employees, it helps ensure that people feel seen and valued. And when managers help individuals on their teams feel that way, they're more likely to be rewarded by employees who become advocates for the department and organization, no matter how long they stay.

**Originally published in January 2022. Reprint H06T9C**

# Harnessing the Power of Age Diversity

*by Megan W. Gerhardt, Josephine Nachemson-Ekwall, and Brandon Fogel*

CONFLICT BETWEEN GENERATIONS is an age-old phenomenon. But at the end of 2019, when the retort "OK, Boomer" went viral, the vitriol—from both young people who said it and older people who opposed it—was pointed and widespread.

The sarcastic phrase was coined by a younger generation to push back on an older one they saw as dismissive and condescending, and it became popular from Korea to New Zealand even though the term "Boomer" is barely used outside of the United States. The retort captured the yawning divide between the generations over seemingly every issue: political activism, climate change, social media, technology, privacy, gender identity.

With five generations together in U.S. workplaces for the first time (Silent Generation, Baby Boomers, Gen X, Millennials, and Gen Z), and similar dynamics playing out in other parts of the world, tensions are mounting. The anger and lack of trust they can cause hurt team performance by limiting collaboration, sparking emotional conflict, and leading to higher employee turnover and lower team performance. And a lack of awareness and understanding of age issues can drive discrimination in hiring and promotion, leading to lawsuit risks.

But many organizations don't take steps to address generational issues. While companies have recently renewed their diversity efforts, only 8% of organizations include age as part of their DEI strategy. And of organizations that do address it, the strategy has often been to simply encourage those of different generations to focus on their similarities or to deny the reality of their differences altogether.

This is a missed opportunity. Age-diverse teams are valuable because they bring together people with complementary abilities, skills, information, and networks. If managed effectively, they can offer better decision-making, more-productive collaboration, and improved overall performance—but only if members are willing to share and learn from their differences. Think of a multigenerational team of product developers, merging the seasoned experience and broad client network of its older members with the fresh perspectives and up-to-date supplier network of its younger ones. Such a group can use its age diversity to build something no generation could on its own.

Take the Open Sustainability Technology Lab at Michigan Technological University, a multigenerational team that developed the first low-cost open-source metal 3D printer. Former director Joshua Pearce credits the team's success to members' willingness to learn from those of other generations. To develop their new product, they needed the technical skills of Gen X faculty, the software wizardry of Millennial graduate students, and the experienced resourcefulness of Boomer researchers. For example, once when a younger team member turned to Amazon to order an urgently needed mechanical component, an older colleague intervened and built it from spare parts more quickly than even Amazon could have delivered it. By combining abilities, the team developed the ability to 3D print in aluminum and steel at a much lower cost than had been possible.

That's why papering over generational differences isn't the answer. Through our work with age-diverse groups in finance, health care, sports, agriculture, and R&D, we've found that a better approach is to help people acknowledge, appreciate, and make use of their differences—just as organizations do with other kinds of

# Idea in Brief

Are tensions between different generations escalating? In organizations, lack of trust between older and younger workers often yields a culture of competition and resentment that leads to real productivity losses. But when age-diverse teams are managed well, members can share a wide array of skills, knowledge, and networks with one another. Organizations already have the means to help

leaders take advantage of these assets: tools that have been used by cross-cultural teams for decades and by DEI initiatives more recently. But these tools are rarely applied to age biases and conflicts. To change that, the authors offer a four-part framework of identifying assumptions, adjusting your lens, taking advantage of differences, and embracing mutual learning.

diversity. Evidence shows that when time-tested DEI tools are used to bridge age divides, they can reduce conflict and generational stereotypes and improve organizational commitment, job satisfaction, employee turnover, and organizational performance.

In our book, *Gentelligence*, we lay out our framework for moving colleagues away from generational conflict and toward a productive embrace of one another's differences. There are four practices involved. The first two, *identify your assumptions* and *adjust your lens*, help overcome false stereotypes. The next two, *take advantage of differences* and *embrace mutual learning*, guide people to share knowledge and expertise so that they can grow together. Each practice also includes an activity to apply its ideas. Teams experiencing generational conflict should start with the first two; the latter two will help groups move beyond simply getting along and leverage the learning and innovation that intergenerational teams can offer.

To introduce the framework, let's look at what makes a generation—and what makes generations different from each other.

## Generations Today

A generation is an age cohort whose members are born during the same period in history and who thus experience significant events and phenomena at similar life stages. These collective

# How Are Generations Defined?

**IN THE U.S. THERE ARE** currently five generations in the workforce: the Silent Generation (typically considered to have been born 1928–1945), Baby Boomers (1946–1964), Gen X (1965–1980), Millennials (1981–1996), and Gen Z (1997–2012).

Each experienced different world events as members came of age, which shaped their views on jobs and careers—and fueled the stereotypes that people have about them. For example, members of the Silent Generation had more prosperity in their adult years than their parents did; they earned a reputation for doing what was asked of them without complaint and building secure lives for their families. Boomers grew up amid economic growth and possibility, relishing long hours at the office and becoming known as workaholics. Gen Xers enjoyed more independence as children than prior generations, leading them to crave greater autonomy and balance in their careers, which then led to their being seen as slackers by their elders. And Millennials, whose development was actively nurtured by their parents from an early age, have come to be seen as expecting rapid career advancement.

Other parts of the world don't necessarily label generations this way; instead, specific age cohorts often acquire a name when their births or childhoods coincide with events of particular culture relevance. Examples include the "little emperors" of China, born during the country's one-child policy; the "born frees" of South Africa, who arrived after apartheid ended; and Kenya's Uhuru ("freedom") Generation, born after the country gained independence. In Sweden cohorts tend to be grouped by decade, but even that can spark tension. Notably, a politician stirred controversy in the early 2000s by coining the name *köttberg*, or "meat mountain," to describe workers born in the 1940s, whom he saw as limiting youth employment.

Around the world, those born recently (such as late Gen Zers and Generation Alpha in the United States) are being shaped by the Covid-19 pandemic. Their early experiences of life, school, and their parents' jobs have mostly been in lockdown and on Zoom. So their ideas and expectations of the workplace will almost surely differ—dramatically—from those of the generations that preceded them.

experiences—say, high unemployment, a population boom, or political change—can shape the group's values and norms in a unique way. Because these formative experiences vary from culture to culture, the specifics of generational makeup vary around the world.

But across geographies, the different outlooks, attitudes, and behaviors of cohorts can lead to conflict. For example, in many countries older workers, who have dominated the workplace for decades, are staying in it longer due to better health and longevity. Younger colleagues, anxious for change and upward mobility, are often impatient for them to move on. And when Boomers and digital natives work side by side, tensions can arise about whose contributions are valued more. If the client database that an older employee developed is replaced by automated software suggested by a younger associate, the older employee may feel that their contribution is being minimized.

These generational frustrations have become even more pronounced during the pandemic. As people of all ages have left their jobs in the so-called Great Resignation, older and younger workers are competing for similar roles. While older workers have more experience, the 35-and-under age groups, according to a recent survey of hiring managers, are seen as having the most relevant education and skills and the best cultural fit for open positions. Even as people flocked online during the pandemic, different generations tended to spend time on different platforms—older people scrolling Facebook, younger ones TikTok—deepening the digital divide. Gen Z employees, meanwhile, have worked remotely for most if not all of their professional lives, leaving many feeling disconnected from coworkers and undervalued by their older teammates. And older generations have adjusted to working from home better than expected, finding the flexibility energizing after a lifetime of long hours at the office.

Many of these tensions—and the media hype around them—have led to a further decline in trust between the generations. The steps we outline in the four practices and activities below are designed to help bridge that gap and move toward better intergenerational cooperation.

## Identify Your Assumptions

The assumptions we make about generational groups (including our own) can hold us back from understanding teammates' true selves as well as the skills, information, and connections they have to offer.

Noticing that we're making these assumptions is the first step to combating them.

Take headlines such as this one from 2019: "Why 'lazy,' 'entitled' millennials can't last 90 days at work." As is often the case, the stereotype on display falls apart on closer inspection. Pew Research Center has found that 70% of Millennials, who are currently aged 26 to 41, stick with their employers for at least 13 months; 69% of Gen Xers stayed that long during the same period of their lives.

Not all biases are blatant enough to make headlines. But even beliefs that we hold at the subconscious level can influence our interactions and our decision-making, often without us realizing it. For example, imagine being asked to nominate a few teammates to lead an Instagram campaign. Who comes to mind? Probably some of your 20-something colleagues. Consciously, you may believe you are choosing those who are the most qualified, most interested, and most able to benefit from the experience. Unconsciously, you may be falling back on deeply embedded assumptions that older people dislike technology or are uninterested in learning anything new.

When it comes to conflict on intergenerational teams, people often rightly suspect there's something age-related going on, but they frequently assume it means something other than what it really does. Let's look at how this played out on one team we studied. At the Fung Fellowship at the University of California, Berkeley, leaders created teams of undergraduates and retirees to collaborate on wellness products for older adults. Initially, these teams ran into several interpersonal challenges. For example, when the retirees didn't respond quickly to texts sent by their younger peers, the students felt that their counterparts weren't taking them or the project seriously. Meanwhile, the retirees resented their teammates' assumptions and seemingly haphazard communication. Work slowed as relations became strained.

Such teams need a tool to recognize the specific age biases they may hold, understand tensions that exist, and head off brewing conflict. We recommend an assumption audit.

**Activity: Assumption Audit**
Challenge employees to spend a week on high alert for age-based assumptions in their daily work. Have them pay attention to their

own actions as well as others'. This might mean noticing, for example, that a team leader dismissed a young employee's request for more responsibility as "entitled" behavior or that you left senior employees out of your meeting on innovation.

After the week has passed, schedule time with the group to discuss their experiences, asking each person to bring at least one observation to the table. These conversations can get charged or lead to defensiveness, but clear ground rules can go a long way in preventing those outcomes. Instruct people to speak about what they heard and saw but not to assume intent: "Input from our younger teammates is dismissed quickly" rather than "Senior leaders dismiss our younger teammates' input because they don't think they have anything to offer." Encourage everyone to be open to feedback and to consider how age-based assumptions—whether containing some truth or absolutely false—might be affecting team cohesion, engagement, and performance.

Plan a follow-up meeting for several weeks later to continue the conversation, ensure accountability, and start building awareness into your everyday work.

When the Fung Fellowship program leaders did their own assumption audit to uncover why the undergraduate-retiree teams were struggling, they found that younger team members had assumed that texts sent after hours would be deemed urgent and would get a quick reply. But older peers thought it went without saying that a text could wait until morning. Identifying these assumptions prompted the team to set shared norms around communication.

## Adjust Your Lens

Recognizing assumptions is important, but teams also need to combat them. Stereotypes often cause us to incorrectly attribute differences to age or to assume ill intent where there is none. *Adjusting your lens* means considering whether the assumptions that you've identified align with the reality of the situation at hand, or whether you've been judging someone's actions and attitudes based only on your frame of reference. Try to understand *why* colleagues from different generations might behave differently than you do. To expand your thinking in that way, use the describe-interpret-evaluate exercise.

### Activity: Describe-Interpret-Evaluate Exercise

Developed in the 1970s to prepare employees to work abroad, this exercise can also help members of age-diverse teams broaden their understanding of one another.

First, have each employee *describe* a frustration they have with someone of a different generation. Next, ask them to think about their initial *interpretation* of the person's behavior. Finally, challenge them to come up with an alternative *evaluation* of your interpretation; they can also ask for contributions from the group.

For example, recently one of us (Megan) conducted a workshop with a group of health care professionals. A nursing manager who identified herself as a Baby Boomer described being annoyed with young patients who used their mobile phones in the middle of a conversation with a nurse or a doctor. Her interpretation was that the patients were—rudely—not paying attention to their caregiving team. When prompted to think of alternative explanations, she looked confused, unable to come up with anything. But her colleagues—mostly younger doctors and nurses—had plenty of ideas: The young patients might be taking notes on the conversation or looking up the pharmacy's hours to make sure they could get their prescriptions before closing. As her teammates offered these insights, the nursing manager's expression changed. She was able to see the behavior in a different light and better appreciate the patients' perspectives. At the same time, her younger colleagues realized how behavior that felt natural to them—like checking a phone mid-conversation—might offend older peers.

## Take Advantage of Differences

Once you've tempered generational tensions by recognizing assumptions and adjusting lenses, you can work on finding productive differences with your colleagues of other generations and ways to benefit from each other's perspectives, knowledge, and networks.

For team members to feel comfortable sharing in this way—bringing up new ideas or conflicting information—they need to feel a certain amount of psychological safety, as the research of Harvard Business School's Amy Edmondson shows. But, as we've seen, perceived generational competition in the workplace, exacerbated by clickbait headlines, has undermined trust. One good way to rebuild it is to hold a roundtable where the team's diverse perspectives can be acknowledged and valued.

### Activity: Intergenerational Roundtable

Leaders of intergenerational teams should set monthly or quarterly meetings to elicit ideas for how to work together more productively and smoothly. There are two stages to the process:

1. *Find common ground and similarities.* While it may seem counterintuitive to focus on commonalities when the goal is to leverage differences, team members must first see themselves as collaborators on a joint mission, rather than competitors. Furthermore, research shows that having a common purpose and goals are vital to team performance. Intergenerational teams can struggle more than most to find that shared ground. So at your first roundtable, ask teammates to work together to answer questions such as "Why does the team exist?" and "What shared goals do we want to accomplish?" This helps team members begin to see themselves as unified in pursuit of the same interests and builds psychological safety. At future sessions, remind them of these discussions.

2. *Invite unique viewpoints.* Next, have each team member respond to the following questions:

   - What are we, as a team, doing well to accomplish these shared goals?

   - What are we doing that is keeping us from reaching these goals?

   - What opportunities should we take advantage of that we currently aren't?

   - If you were in charge, what would you continue, stop, or start doing?

Your aim is not to come to neat conclusions but to surface new ideas that might have been dismissed or unvoiced in the past. Different views will inevitably surface, and some conflict may even erupt—that's all right. Just keep bringing the conversation back to the team's shared goals and emphasize that differences of opinion are valued contributions toward your common success.

Aaron Hornbrook, a customer service manager and vice president at Wells Fargo we've interviewed, holds monthly roundtable meetings with his multigenerational team. At the beginning of each, Hornbrook reminds everyone that their mission is to help customers with their application- and account-related questions and that success will require both trust and willingness to listen to the perspectives of the entire group. His efforts have borne fruit: For example, his Millennial and Gen Z employees feel comfortable voicing their concerns about mental health in the workplace—a subject previously considered taboo by some of their older colleagues. These conversations helped Hornbrook and other senior colleagues understand why paid-time-off requests had spiked recently and prompted them to find ways to reduce employee anxiety, including by requiring supervisors to hold one-on-one meetings with direct reports in conference rooms rather than at their desks. As a result, team members of all generations became more supportive of people taking mental health days.

By creating a space for team members to discuss how the group functions, managers demonstrate that all perspectives are valued.

## Embrace Mutual Learning

Finally, to fully reap the benefits of intergenerational teams, members must believe that they have something to learn from colleagues in different age cohorts. The ultimate goal is mutual learning: peers of all ages teaching and learning from one another in an ongoing loop.

One way to encourage this is with formal mentoring initiatives. While traditional mentoring programs (older colleagues teaching younger ones) exist at many organizations, a number of top companies—including GE, Deloitte, PwC, Cisco, and Procter & Gamble—have developed "reverse mentoring" programs, where younger people teach older peers new skills, typically around technology. We suggest that companies and even managers of small teams combine both approaches into two-way "mutual mentoring." Research shows that such programs support employees' development of competencies and skills and increase both individual involvement and collective motivation.

Mutual learning can also happen organically when people of different generations have good relationships and are on the lookout for opportunities. BuildWitt Media, a digital storytelling firm we've studied, helps its clients in the construction and mining industries attract great talent. Its founder and CEO is 26-year-old Aaron Witt; its president, Dan Briscoe, is 53. While cross-generational learning was never an explicit reason for their partnership, they have come to value how Briscoe's 30 years of experience in leadership, sales, and marketing complement Witt's impulsive energy, sense of business trends, and lifelong immersion in mobile media. For example, Briscoe credits Witt with teaching him to look beyond academic degrees and GPA when hiring and to consider leadership potential and alignment with culture and values in addition to a work portfolio. Witt says Briscoe is good at relating to clients and putting deals together. This partnership, they agree, has led to rapid growth and the opportunity to diversify their services.

### Activity: Mutual Mentoring

To start building a mentorship culture on your team, create an informal mutual mentoring network. Begin by asking team members of all ages what they want to learn and what they want to teach. Potential teachers can be surprisingly shy when it comes to their expertise; it may help if you make suggestions about what you see as their strengths.

Identify where there are natural connections: employees who are versed in TikTok and those who want to learn to create selfie videos, or employees who have an established roster of clients and those who want to expand their networks. While not all pairings need to be cross-generational, make sure all generations are represented in both the learner and the instructor groups.

Once you have some pairings ready, hold a kickoff meeting with the entire team and ask four to six mentors to present briefly on their area of expertise. Encourage people to reach out to the mentors whose skills they want to learn. Often the energy of the meeting itself will spur connections, but you can also send monthly nudges to remind the team to keep questions flowing.

Even this kind of informal network can help to build a culture of cross-generational learning.

---

"OK, Boomer," "Gen X cynics," "entitled Millennials," and "Gen Z snowflakes." We have become so entrenched in generational name-calling—or, conversely, so focused on downplaying the differences that do exist—that we have forgotten there is strength in age diversity. Especially at a time when we are wrestling with so many changes to the way we work, it's incumbent on leaders to embrace intergenerational teams as a key piece of the DEI puzzle and to frame them as an opportunity to be seized rather than a threat to be managed.

---

# Is Generational Prejudice Seeping into Your Workplace?

*by Kristi DePaul and Vasundhara Sawhney*

The year is 2005. YouTube has just launched, and social media usage is on the rise. Mariah Carey and Gwen Stefani are vying for the top song of the year. The first cohort of Millennials is stepping into the workforce. And the business world has plenty to celebrate: The economy is booming, job offers are plentiful and competitive, and technology is advancing faster than ever.

It sounds like a youthful happily ever after. But there was a plot twist: Millennials were eyed warily by their employers and colleagues.

Report after report emphasized how much Baby Boomers and Gen Xers needed to change to accommodate this new generation of lazy, entitled, and disloyal workers and how these young folks would disrupt the workplace as we knew it. The media latched on to these generalizations, reporting that Millennials wanted more "me" time on the job, only took "yes" for an answer, and let their parents assume a peculiarly active role in their professional lives.

As a result, company leaders and senior employees did change, creating processes and policies based on these beliefs. Ping-Pong tables and beer on tap became priorities, constant feedback the gold standard, work-life balance more important than meaningful career progression.

Did these changes actually help Millennials succeed at work? Hardly. While some companies reported lower turnover rates after introducing flexible work schedules, aggressive engagement policies, and wellness programs, the "me me me" generation was actually burning out. Turns out it was filled with workaholics; many discontented Millennials embraced side hustles amid the burgeoning gig economy and the uncertainty of the Covid-19 pandemic. (And no, those Ping-Pong tables weren't necessary.)

As Millennials ourselves, we have been subjected to pervasive stereotyping ("I'm sure you prefer Slack over email") and condescending assumptions ("You've been here for two years. Time to move on?"). If you're part of this generation, you've probably experienced bias like this too. Workers of all generations have—when it comes to our supposed differences from each other, there are plenty of stereotypes to go around.

This made us wonder: Does intergenerational anxiety stem from *actual* differences? Or is it created by the mere *belief* that certain disparities exist? And if it's the latter, what can we do to thwart those stereotypes before we create mismatched workplaces for generations to come?

## Why Generational Biases Exist at Work

Beliefs about generations have long provided a flawed but convenient framework for managerial thinking and decision-making. Our research for this article uncovered a few reasons they persist.

### We put things in buckets to make sense of them
According to Michael Kramer, former chair of the department of communication at the University of Oklahoma, "Humans naturally seek simplified explanations for their own and others' behavior through a process of sensemaking, especially during uncertain times. Constructing and adopting stereotypes is one way of doing that."

Bobby Duffy, a professor and the author of *The Generation Myth: Why When You're Born Matters Less Than You Think*, agrees. "We like stories about who we are and who we're not, and we like to categorize everything into what it is and what it's not," he told us. These stories are appealing, especially when they're vivid and memorable, with labels and anecdotes behind them. "And that's certainly what's happened with generational labels," he added.

All of this can make us feel closer to colleagues of our generation. "We feel that when we are born matters because there is a sense of connection to our peers . . . They have gone through what we have gone through. It feels intuitive. And it works really well as shorthand communication in headlines or when we want to sum up complex things in simple labels," Duffy said.

Managers who are nervous or unsure about leading a new age cohort—particularly when the media is putting them on high alert—may rely on generational labels as shortcuts for engaging and attracting those workers. Duffy noted that leaders sometimes use stereotypes as scapegoats when something isn't working. "When you believe that it's not your fault as an employer—that it's just this weird generation coming into the workforce and placing unreasonable demands on you—you shift the blame onto them" instead of understanding and addressing the root issue.

## Rosy retrospection plagues us

Cognitive psychologist Gordon Bower found that our memories are reconstructed when we recall them—a process prone to manipulation and errors. Various types of memory bias can affect our decision-making in both positive and negative ways. Rosy retrospection, or declinism, is one such bias: It refers to our tendency to minimize the negatives of the past, leading us to view it more positively than the present.

Duffy says that, as a result, we think things used to be better than they are now and believe everything is going downhill. "Coupled with generational thinking, we feel the current situation is dreadful; clearly, the new generation is at fault and will change everything," he explains wryly. When we look for someone to blame, a new cohort could, conveniently, fit the bill.

But if you feel that young workers today are being too demanding (whether about wanting better tech infrastructure or sporting tattoos and beards at work), you're probably forgetting that you, too, were insistent and intent on forging your identity at that age. Or as one illustrative example proffered: "The hippies of the late 1960s became the dress-for-success yuppies of the 1980s."

## Employers are vying for talent in any way they can

Consider Google, with its nap pods, on-site laundry service, free snacks, and colorful beanbag chairs. What began as a data-driven recruitment and retention strategy—projecting the company's "cool quotient" to encourage a robust applicant pool and lengthier employee tenures—soon became an industry benchmark that others measured branding efforts against.

More recently, companies have used popular insights to "seem less square." They're marketing themselves as culturally diverse (Millennials expect a diverse workplace), providing collaborative environments (Millennials work better in groups than alone) and flexible work schedules (Gen Zers love work-life balance), and keeping their Instagram profiles up to date (both generations like that one) to attract younger people. Firms are also conducting extensive employer brand surveys to reveal the priorities of specific generations—yet many may not be unique to any age group, like better compensation packages and meaningful work.

### Generational stereotypes have created a cottage industry

From books to podcasts to consultancies, there are any number of lucrative reasons to assert that generational differences do, indeed, exist and are central to the workplace. "There's a whole industry around generations," Cort Rudolph, an industrial and organizational psychologist and faculty member at Saint Louis University whose research focuses on work and aging, told us.

Because managers are led to believe they must adapt their approaches for different generations—and are unsure about how to do that—they often seek help that can provide insights and guidance. As a result, "companies go out and hire generational experts to come in and clean up intergenerational conflicts," said Rudolph.

And it's not cheap. As of a few years ago, some consultants were charging $20,000 to $30,000 per hour, and Source Global Research estimated that U.S. organizations spent $60 million to $70 million on generational consulting in 2015 alone. The long-term success of such efforts remains to be seen (we're still debating if Millennials will ever get the workplace they want), but meanwhile generational consulting related to Gen Z has become popular.

## Moving Beyond Generational Thinking

But is it really so bad if companies try to leverage popular insights to win over every generation at work? Well, possibly yes. "We're basing a lot of practice decisions, a lot of policies, a lot of approaches in the workplace on pretty shaky science," Rudolph explained. And it can negatively affect employees. In fact, for this article we posted a LinkedIn poll to ask people if being part of a generation negatively influences how they're treated at work. Sixty percent of respondents said it did.

Often what's happening—which is less intentional than overt ageism—is reflected in organizational practices that, while appearing benign, aren't applied to everyone equally. Rudolph offered an example: the popular narrative that people from younger generations want more flexibility. "As a manager, I'm going to read that and then afford different levels of flexibility to people based on their age. What results is a policy that seems to be grounded in what a certain subset of the population wants—when in reality, *everybody* values flexibility."

Such beliefs can influence everything from how new teammates are onboarded, to how they are trained or mentored, to even how teams collaborate and communicate—and that breadth can pose great risk to organizations' age inclusivity and employee performance. One experiment found that trainers assigned to teach someone a computer-related task had lower expectations and provided worse training when they believed the person was older.

So, how do we design policies and processes that protect us from ageist behaviors, rather than relying on assumptions or stereotypes?

### Consider other explanations for employee similarities and differences

"It's really difficult to separate out what is actually a generation from other types of influences that co-occur with time," noted Rudolph. Each of us has more in common with our older and younger counterparts than we might realize, which can be attributed to *life cycle effects*, or how we grow and change as we age. For example, younger professionals—who are typically less tied down by family obligations—are more likely to experiment with their careers and take risks to find the right fit, as compared with older workers, who are more established in their careers. Ironically, a report from the U.S. Bureau of Labor Statistics shows that Boomers did as much job hopping in their twenties as Millennials at that age.

There are other kinds of effects that influence us too. A 2020 report found that people born in the same year or span of years may share some similarities (*cohort effects*), though they may have very different experiences and outlooks depending on social and economic factors or geographic location. People are also influenced by *period effects*, or events and changes (a pandemic, a war, a recession) that impact everyone at a given point in time. Attributing someone's behavior to one effect when it's due more to another effect can lead to misunderstandings.

For example, Millennials and Gen Zers are known for the stereotype that they switch jobs quickly. That might seem to be a cohort effect—young people today like to job hop, perhaps because they're disloyal to employers. But consider that both generations spent their formative years in a recession—a period effect. Members with access to higher-paying roles and industry connections or with the ability to live in a region with ample job opportunities may be doing fine. But many others haven't accumulated wealth the way their predecessors did and have comparatively sluggish earning trajectories. They've also started fewer businesses due to unfavorable economic conditions. These factors, combined with pension plans becoming outmoded and the fact that significant raises usually don't come from advancing in one's current company, have led many younger workers to job hop to seek higher wages—so they can devote more to retirement savings.

### Recognize that employees' needs are often universal

Jessica Kriegel, a workplace culture expert and the author of *Unfairly Labeled: How Your Workplace Can Benefit from Ditching Generational Stereotypes*, described to us a town hall meeting gone awry when a CEO stated that Millennials value work-life balance more than compensation. What he believed to be an innocuous comment—a compliment, even—caused an uproar. Employees of all ages complained to HR.

"Millennials were adamant that salary mattered to them and were concerned the organization had offered them less as a result of this work-life belief," Kriegel explained. "And older employees insisted that work-life balance was important to them as well. People generally have a negative reaction to being told who they are and what they value."

So, if managers and leaders should stop using generations as a framework for customizing policies, what should they use instead?

Rudolph suggests focusing on actual, identifiable, and relevant differences by adopting a life-span perspective on aging at work—that is, focusing on the differences between and changes within employees as they age.

For example, you might base your policies on the assumption that only Millennials care about work-life balance, autonomy, or flexible working hours. But when you consider a life-span perspective, you realize that any caregiver would find those policies attractive, irrespective of generation. Offering tailor-made policies isn't just an inefficient use of resources, as some employees may not want them; it also ties up resources that would be highly valued by those who actually need them.

### Consider societal changes when crafting policies

Task- or work-environment-related changes must address larger societal trends and universal factors, such as pay transparency (employees want to lessen the gender pay gap) or better work-life integration (work isn't the only thing employees want to do with their time).

For example, many couples are choosing to delay having children or not carry children themselves. In response, Zomato—India's biggest food-delivery app—introduced a 26-week parental leave that applies to all employees, including surrogate or adoptive parents as well as same-sex parents. "The needs of our people are more specific to their life stages and the roles they play at work and at home, as compared to the generation they belong to," Daminee Sawhney, the company's vice president, human resources and operations, explained.

Naturally, such policies shouldn't be created in a vacuum. Zomato considers a combination of its culture and the feedback it receives from employees about what they expect from the organization in the long term. "We don't rely on generational studies or consultants to guide us. Instead, we enable our people to operate from a space of accountability and trust and believe in continually assessing and abandoning practices that no longer serve us as a collective," Sawhney added.

The rise in remote work is another example of a societal change that is valuable irrespective of someone's generation. SAP in India designed its work-from-home policy in 2013 in response to employee proposals. The policy has evolved through the pandemic and has been honed to address the future of work.

"Pledge to Flex is an excellent example of how we have taken perspectives of employees representing various personas on what flexibility and hybrid work meant to them and has stood the test of time," Shraddhanjali Rao, the company's head of HR, told us. "Today, we have a playbook that respects individuality and empowers our employees to choose their way of hybrid working, keeping their teams and business context in mind."

Like the shift to working from home, some societal changes will be easy to identify and difficult to ignore. Others will require paying more attention to how new governmental policies might impact workers in your industry or to what other organizations offer employees, such as fertility benefits or tuition reimbursement. Maintaining an open internal dialogue within company forums can help leaders to further identify the supports that are most valued by their workforce.

The recommendations we've described may not entirely rid your organization of generational biases. But they can help you understand when focusing on generational differences might not be helpful. Only then can you begin building programs and processes that meaningfully support an age-diverse workforce.

**Originally published in March 2022. Reprint** BG2201

# The C-Suite Skills That Matter Most

*by Raffaella Sadun, Joseph Fuller, Stephen Hansen, and PJ Neal*

**FOR A LONG TIME,** whenever companies wanted to hire a CEO or another key executive, they knew what to look for: somebody with technical expertise, superior administrative skills, and a track record of successfully managing financial resources. When courting outside candidates to fill those roles, they often favored executives from companies such as GE, IBM, and P&G and from professional-services giants such as McKinsey and Deloitte, which had a reputation for cultivating those skills in their managers.

That practice now feels like ancient history. So much has changed during the past two decades that companies can no longer assume that leaders with traditional managerial pedigrees will succeed in the C-suite. Today firms need to hire executives who are able to motivate diverse, technologically savvy, and global workforces; who can play the role of corporate statesperson, dealing effectively with constituents ranging from sovereign governments to influential NGOs; and who can rapidly and effectively apply their skills in a new company, in what may be an unfamiliar industry, and often with colleagues in the C-suite whom they didn't previously know.

These changes present a phenomenal challenge for executive recruitment, because the capabilities required of top leaders include new and often "softer" skills that are rarely explicitly recognized or fostered in the corporate world. Simply put, it's getting harder and less prudent to rely on traditional indicators of managerial potential.

What should organizations do to face this challenge? A critical first step is to develop greater clarity about what it now takes for C-suite executives to succeed. Yes, the range of necessary skills appears to have expanded—but how exactly? For example, what does the term "soft skills" really mean? And to what extent does the need to hire executives with more-expansive skills vary across organizations?

Remarkably, even though almost every aspect of leadership has been scrutinized in recent years, rigorous evidence on these crucial points is scant. To find out more—about the capabilities that are now in demand, how those have changed over time, and what adjustments companies are making to their process for selecting candidates—we recently analyzed data from Russell Reynolds Associates, one of the world's premier executive-search firms. Russell Reynolds and its competitors play an essential role in managerial labor markets: 80% to 90% of the *Fortune* 250 and FTSE 100 companies use the services of such firms when making a succession decision that involves a choice among candidates. (Disclosure: Russell Reynolds has recently conducted executive searches for Harvard Business Publishing, which publishes *Harvard Business Review*.)

For our research, Russell Reynolds gave us unprecedented access to nearly 5,000 job descriptions that it had developed in collaboration with its clients from 2000 to 2017. The data was sufficient to study expectations not just for the CEO but also for four other key leaders in the C-suite: the chief financial officer, the chief information officer, the head of human resources, and the chief marketing officer. To our knowledge, researchers had never before analyzed such a comprehensive collection of senior-executive job descriptions. (For more about how we worked with the data, see the sidebar "About the Research.")

Our study yielded a variety of insights. Chief among them is this: Over the past two decades, companies have significantly redefined

## Idea in Brief

**The Shift**

It's no longer safe to assume that leaders with traditional managerial pedigrees will succeed in the C-suite. An analysis of executive-search data shows that companies today are prioritizing social skills above technical know-how, expertise in financial stewardship, and other qualifications.

**The Explanation**

Large companies today have increasingly complex operations, heavier reliance on technology, more workforce diversity, and greater public accountability for their behavior. Leading under those circumstances requires superior listening and communication skills and an ability to relate well to multiple constituencies.

**The Path Forward**

To succeed in the years ahead, companies will have to figure out how to effectively evaluate the social skills of job candidates. They will also need to make such skills an integral part of their talent-management strategies.

the roles of C-suite executives. The traditional capabilities mentioned earlier—notably the management of financial and operational resources—remain highly relevant. But when companies today search for top leaders, especially new CEOs, they attribute less importance to those capabilities than they used to and instead prioritize one qualification above all others: strong social skills. (See the exhibit "Help wanted: CEOs who are good with people.")

When we refer to "social skills," we mean certain specific capabilities, including a high level of self-awareness, the ability to listen and communicate well, a facility for working with different types of people and groups, and what psychologists call "theory of mind"— the capacity to infer how others are thinking and feeling. The magnitude of the shift in recent years toward these capabilities is most significant for CEOs but also pronounced for the four other C-suite roles we studied.

Our analysis revealed that social skills are particularly important in settings where productivity hinges on effective communication, as it invariably does in the large, complex, and skill-intensive enterprises

## About the Research

**THIS ARTICLE IS BASED ON** a rich data set drawn from almost 5,000 job descriptions compiled by Russell Reynolds Associates and companies conducting searches for various C-suite positions. Translating that data into variables that were amenable to quantitative analysis was no easy feat, because the job descriptions did not follow a standard structure or contain standard content. Our approach involved two steps.

First we defined a distinctive set of skill requirements that were relevant for chief executives. We started by combing through the U.S. Department of Labor's O*NET database (a repository of information about more than 1,000 occupations) to see what skills were listed for "chief executive" roles. We then sorted those into six clusters that included similar tasks: managing financial and material resources; monitoring corporate performance; tending to human resources; handling administrative tasks; processing and using complex information; and exercising social skills.

Our second step was to determine the extent to which each job description provided by Russell Reynolds was semantically similar to each O*NET skills cluster.

Both steps relied on a model of managerial language that we developed by applying cutting-edge machine-learning techniques (word2vec) to a corpus composed of every *Harvard Business Review* article published since the magazine's inception in 1922.

that employ executive search firms. In such organizations, CEOs and other senior leaders can't limit themselves to performing routine operational tasks. They also have to spend a significant amount of time interacting with others and enabling coordination—by communicating information, facilitating the exchange of ideas, building and overseeing teams, and identifying and solving problems.

Intriguingly, the evolution of skills requirements in the C-suite parallels developments in the workforce as a whole. At all employment levels today, more and more jobs require highly developed social skills. Harvard's David Deming, among others, has demonstrated that such jobs have grown at a faster rate than the labor market as a whole—and that compensation for them is growing faster than average.

## Help wanted: CEOs who are good with people

*Since 2007, companies advertising C-suite openings have increasingly emphasized the importance of social skills and deemphasized operational expertise.*

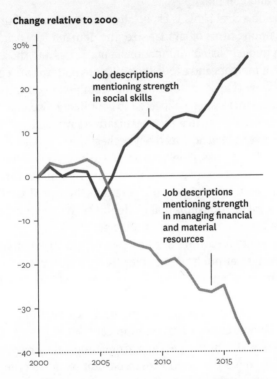

**Change relative to 2000**

Job descriptions mentioning strength in social skills

Job descriptions mentioning strength in managing financial and material resources

*Note:* Job descriptions were for nearly 5,000 C-suite positions advertised by the executive-search firm Russell Reynolds Associates. The data points were estimated in a regression model that controls for industry differences and other variables. The coefficients after 2007 are significantly different from zero across both skill clusters.

Why is this shift toward social skills taking place? And what implications does it have for executive development, CEO succession planning, and the organization of the C-suite? This article offers some preliminary thoughts.

## The Chief Reasons for Change

We've identified two main drivers of the growing demand for social skills.

### Firm size and complexity

The focus on social skills is especially evident in large firms. Additionally, among firms of similar size, the demand for social skills is greater at publicly listed multinational enterprises and those that are involved in mergers and acquisitions. These patterns are consistent with the view that in larger and more complex organizations, top managers are increasingly expected to coordinate disparate and specialized knowledge, match the organization's problems with people who can solve them, and effectively orchestrate internal communication. For all those tasks, it helps to be able to interact well with others.

But the importance of social skills in large companies arises from more than just the complexity of operations there. It also reflects the web of critical relationships that leaders at such firms must cultivate and maintain with outside constituencies.

The diversity and number of those relationships can be daunting. Executives at public companies have to worry not only about product markets but also about capital markets. They need to brief analysts, woo asset managers, and address the business press. They must respond to various kinds of regulators across multiple jurisdictions. They're expected to communicate well with key customers and suppliers. During mergers and acquisitions, they have to attend carefully to constituents who are important to closing the transaction and supporting the post-merger integration. Highly developed social skills are critical to success in all those arenas.

### Information-processing technologies

"The more we automate information handling," management guru Peter Drucker wrote several decades ago, "the more we will have to create opportunities for effective communication." That has turned out to be prescient: Companies that rely significantly on information-processing technologies today also tend to be those that need leaders with especially strong social skills.

Here's why. Increasingly, in every part of the organization, when companies automate routine tasks, their competitiveness hinges on capabilities that computer systems simply don't have—things such as judgment, creativity, and perception. In technologically intensive firms, where automation is widespread, leaders have to align a heterogeneous workforce, respond to unexpected events, and manage conflict in the decision-making process, all of which are best done by managers with strong social skills.

Moreover, most companies today rely on many of the same technological platforms—Amazon Web Services, Facebook, Google, Microsoft, Salesforce, Workday. That means they have less opportunity to differentiate themselves on the basis of tangible technological investments alone. When every major competitor in a market leverages the same suite of tools, leaders need to distinguish themselves through superior management of the people who use those tools. That requires them to be top-notch communicators in every regard, able both to devise the right messages and to deliver them with empathy.

In sum, as more tasks are entrusted to technology, workers with superior social skills will be in demand at all levels and will command a premium in the labor market.

## Other Factors

Our research suggests that the growing interest in social skills is being spurred by two additional drivers. These are harder to quantify, but they nonetheless may play an important role in the shift that's taking place.

### Social media and networking technologies
Historically, CEOs didn't attract much popular notice, nor did they seek the limelight. While other businesspeople, investors, and members of the business press paid attention to them, the public generally did not, except in the cases of "celebrity" CEOs such as GE's Jack Welch, Sony's Akio Morita, and Chrysler's Lee Iacocca.

That era is over. As companies move away from shareholder primacy and focus more broadly on stakeholder capitalism, CEOs and other senior leaders are expected to be public figures. They're obliged not only to interact with an increasingly broad range of internal and external constituencies but to do so personally and transparently and accountably. No longer can they rely on support functions—the corporate communications team, the government relations department, and so forth—to take care of all those relationships.

Furthermore, top leaders must manage interactions in real time, thanks to the increasing prevalence of both social media (which can capture and publicize missteps nearly instantaneously) and network platforms such as Slack and Glassdoor (which allow employees to widely disseminate information and opinions about their colleagues and bosses).

In the past, too, executives were expected to be able to explain and defend everything from their business strategies to their HR practices. But they did so in a controlled environment, at a time and a place of management's choosing. Now they must be constantly attuned to how their decisions are perceived by various audiences. Failing to achieve their intended purposes with even a handful of employees or other constituents can be damaging.

So social skills matter greatly. The occupants of the C-suite need to be adroit at communicating spontaneously and anticipating how their words and actions will play beyond the immediate context.

### Diversity and inclusion

Another new challenge for CEOs and other senior leaders is dealing with issues of diversity and inclusion—publicly, empathetically, and proactively. That, too, demands strong social skills, particularly theory of mind. Executives who possess that perceptiveness about the mental states of others can move more easily among various employee groups, make them feel heard, and represent their interests within the organization, to the board of directors, and to outside constituencies. More importantly, they can nurture an environment in which diverse talent thrives.

## New Areas for Focus

Given the critical role that social skills play in leadership success today, companies will need to refocus on the following areas as they hire and cultivate new leaders.

### Systematically building social skills

Traditionally, boards and senior executives have cultivated future leaders by rotating them through critical departments and functions, posting them to various geographic locations, and putting them through executive development programs. It was assumed that the best way to prepare promising managers for a future in the C-suite was to have them develop deep competence in a variety of administrative and operational roles.

With this model, evaluating success and failure was reasonably straightforward. Processes ran smoothly or they didn't; results were achieved or they weren't. Social skills mattered, of course: As up-and-comers moved through functions and geographies, their ability to quickly form constructive relationships with colleagues, customers, regulators, and suppliers affected their performance. But such skills were considered something of a bonus. They were a means to achieving operational objectives (a prerequisite for advancement) and were seldom evaluated in an explicit, systematic, and objective way.

Companies today better appreciate the importance of social skills in executive performance, but they've made little progress in devising processes for evaluating a candidate's proficiency in those skills and determining aptitude for further growth. Few companies invest in training to improve the interviewing skills of staffers involved in recruiting—least of all senior executives or independent directors, who are presumed to have the background and perspective necessary to make sound judgments.

Getting references is also problematic: Companies typically conduct senior-level searches with a high degree of confidentiality, both to protect themselves (a leak could cost them the best prospect) and to protect the candidates (who might not want their employers to know that they're open to job offers). Moreover, the people conducting C-suite interviews and those providing references are likely to be part of the same small, homogeneous networks as most of the candidates, which significantly heightens the risk of bias in the decision-making process. For example, board members tend to support candidates who are referred by friends or have backgrounds similar to their own. They might mistakenly assume that those individuals possess broadly applicable social skills simply because they connected easily with them in interviews.

To better evaluate social skills, some companies now run psychometric assessments or simulations. Psychometric tests (which are designed to measure personality traits and behavioral style) can help establish whether someone is outgoing and comfortable with strangers, but they shed little light on how effective that person will be when interacting with various groups. Simulation exercises, for their part, have been used for some time to evaluate how individuals respond to challenging circumstances, but they're usually designed around a specific scenario, such as a product-integrity crisis or the arrival of an activist investor on the scene. Simulations are best at assessing candidates' administrative and technical skills in such situations, rather than their ability to coordinate teams or interact spontaneously with diverse constituencies. Even so, these exercises are not widely used, because of the time and money required to run them well.

In their executive development programs, companies today need a systematic approach to building and evaluating social skills. They may even need to prioritize them over the "hard" skills that managers presently favor because they're so easy to assess. Companies should place high-potential leaders in positions that oblige them to interact with various employee populations and external constituencies and then closely monitor their performance in those roles.

### Assessing social skills innovatively

The criteria that companies have traditionally used to size up candidates for C-suite positions—such as work history, technical qualifications, and career trajectory—are of limited value in assessing social skills. Companies will need to create new tools if they are to establish an objective basis for evaluating and comparing people's abilities in this realm. They can act either independently or in conjunction with the professional-services firms that support them, but in either case they'll need to custom-design solutions to serve their particular needs.

Although appropriate tools have yet to be developed for searches at the highest echelons of organizations, considerable innovation is underway when it comes to ascertaining the skills of lower-level job seekers and placing them in the right positions. Companies such as Eightfold and Gloat, for example, are using artificial intelligence to improve matching between candidates and employers. New custom tools are also being used to identify skill adjacencies and to create internal talent marketplaces, helping companies assign qualified employees to important tasks more quickly. The underlying algorithms rely on huge data sets, which poses a technological challenge, but this approach holds promise for executive recruiting.

Similarly, pymetrics, among other companies, is mining world-class behavioral research to see how particular candidates fit with an organization or a specific position. Such an approach has proved useful in evaluating a broad array of soft skills and in reducing bias in recruiting. Recent academic work shows the utility of tapping into behavioral research: Harvard's Ben Weidmann and David Deming, for example, have found that the Reading the Mind in the Eyes Test, a well-established measure of social intelligence, can effectively predict the performance of individuals in team settings. If companies develop new tests based on the same design principles, they and their boards of directors should be able to gain a fuller and more objective understanding of the social skills of C-suite candidates.

### Emphasizing social skills development at all levels

Companies that rely on outside hiring to find executives with superior social skills are playing a dangerous game. For one thing, competition for such people will become fierce. For another, it's inherently risky to put an outsider—even someone carefully vetted—in a senior role. Companies thus will benefit from a "grow your own" approach that allows internal up-and-comers to hone and demonstrate a range of interpersonal abilities.

### Assessing the collective social skills in the C-suite

Increasingly, boards of directors and company executives will need to develop and evaluate the social skills of not only individual leaders but the C-suite as a whole. Weakness or ineptitude on the part of any one person on the team will have a systems effect on the group—and especially the CEO. Companies recognize this: Social skills are gaining in relative importance in the search criteria for all five of the executive positions we studied. Moreover, as CEOs continue playing a bigger role in constituency and personnel management, the responsibilities within the C-suite may be reconfigured, and other executives will need strong social skills too.

## The Way Forward

As we've established, companies still value C-suite executives with traditional administrative and operational skills. But they're increasingly on the lookout for people with highly developed social skills—especially if their organizations are large, complex, and technologically intensive.

Will companies, however, actually succeed in making different kinds of hires? That's an open question. The answer will depend in part on whether they can figure out how to effectively evaluate the social skills of job candidates, and whether they decide to make the cultivation of social skills an integral component of their talent-management strategies.

In our view, companies are going to have to do both those things to remain competitive. To that end, they should encourage business schools and other educators to place more emphasis on social skills in their MBA and executive-level curricula, and they should challenge search firms and other intermediaries to devise innovative mechanisms for identifying and assessing candidates.

Companies themselves will also have to do things differently. In recruiting and evaluating outside talent, they must prioritize social skills. The same is true when it comes to measuring the performance of current executives and setting their compensation. In addition, firms should make strong social skills a criterion for promotion, and they should task supervisors with nurturing such skills in high-potential subordinates.

In the years ahead, some companies may focus on trying to better identify and hire leaders with "the right stuff"; others may pay more attention to executive training and retention. But no matter what approach they adopt, it's clear that to succeed in an increasingly challenging business environment, they'll have to profoundly rethink their current practices.

**Originally published in July–August 2022. Reprint** S22041

# Your Company Needs a Space Strategy. Now.

*by Matthew Weinzierl, Prithwiraj (Raj) Choudhury, Tarun Khanna, Alan MacCormack, and Brendan Rosseau*

IN THE EARLY 2000s, AS THE U.S. SPACE SHUTTLE PROGRAM was winding down, the government's policy on space moved away from its model of flowing all money and decisions through NASA and the Department of Defense. Instead, it began to allow privately funded companies to compete for public-sector contracts. The Commercial Orbital Transportation Services program (commonly known as COTS) and its successors, for example, gave private companies fixed-price contracts, rather than the cost-plus contracts typically used in the space sector, to provide services to resupply the International Space Station.

That change spurred the growth of rocket launch companies like Blue Origin, Sierra Space, and SpaceX, which have leveraged advances in microelectronics and computing over the past several decades to drive down the costs of getting satellites (the most common payload) into space by making them smaller, lighter, and more powerful. Today the cost of launching a satellite using SpaceX's Falcon Heavy is less than 8% of the cost of launching one before 2000, before private companies were invited to compete. And projections for SpaceX's next vehicle, Starship, hover in the single-digit millions of dollars. Given a payload capacity of 150 metric tons, that could bring costs per kilogram down to less than $100.

At the same time, the proliferation of smartphones and other satellite-connected devices has driven demand for those satellites. Jeff Bezos (who founded Blue Origin) and Elon Musk (who founded SpaceX) built their personal fortunes on the industries created by technological advances, and they are now providing abundant and patient seed capital to their space startups.

The billionaires don't have the field all to themselves. Venture capital has flowed into the sector as well, increasing from less than $1 billion in the early 2000s to more than $15 billion in 2021, according to space consultancy Bryce-Tech. That has helped fund more than 100 startups that are developing smaller rockets to provide bespoke launch services—placing satellites in precise orbital locations, for example, and making space accessible to customers whose launch needs are unsuitable for the "rideshare" model of the larger rockets. (In that model, many satellites share the cost of a launch and are released together; then they independently navigate to their various destinations.) Riding this wave of more-affordable access to space are hundreds of young satellite companies, each developing innovative technologies that take advantage of the unique opportunities and environment of space.

The result is that space is becoming an important source of value for businesses across diverse sectors—including agriculture, pharmaceuticals, tourism, and consumer goods. Businesses such as Apple, Amazon Web Services, General Motors, John Deere, Merck, and many more are already making moves. And Microsoft, which in 2020 launched Azure Space, a platform connecting "the possibilities of space with the power of the cloud," has said that every one of its enterprise customers could benefit from space.

What are the opportunities for your company? To answer that question, consider the four ways in which using space could create value: data, capabilities, resources, and markets. For most companies thinking about their space strategy over the next five to 10 years—whether as providers of space services or as customers

## Idea in Brief

**The Situation**

Space is becoming a potential source of value for businesses across a range of sectors, including agriculture, pharmaceuticals, consumer goods, and tourism.

**The Explanation**

Rocket launch companies like SpaceX, Blue Origin, and Sierra Space have leveraged advances in microelectronics and computing to drive down the costs of getting to space.

**The Opportunities**

This article examines four ways that companies can create value using space: through data, capabilities, resources, and markets. For most companies thinking about their space strategy over the next five to 10 years, data will be the dominant focus. The other areas hold promise for later exploration. Companies engaging with commercial space should be willing to experiment and look for partners.

of them—data will be the dominant focus. Those looking further ahead, though, will want to explore the value to be gained from the others as well.

## Data: Learning from and through Space

The best-known uses of space involve data—either gathering data *from* space about what is happening on Earth or transmitting data *through* space from one part of the world to another. These uses are already well established, but their reach is expanding.

The now classic example of how space can deliver value for businesses is the Global Positioning System, or GPS. Originally created to provide position, navigation, and timing data for the U.S. military, GPS has become critical to the world economy. A 2019 study sponsored by the National Institute of Standards and Technology found that since GPS's services were opened to the private sector in 1983, GPS has generated roughly $1.4 trillion in economic benefits for U.S. industries, including agriculture, transportation, energy, and consumer goods. About 90% of the benefits have been realized in the past 10 years. And altogether new kinds of companies, including rideshare services such as Uber and Lyft, have been built on its back.

GPS was just the start. Today the private sector has access to an increasingly broad, diverse, and powerful set of space-based data and services at ever more cost-effective prices. Take remote-sensing satellites, which use a suite of sensors to generate information about our planet's surface almost in real time. Companies are increasingly turning to remote-sensing companies for data that will inform business decisions. Whether it's tracking the number of cars parked in retail locations, detecting costly and environmentally damaging methane leaks from natural-gas wells, or assessing soil type and moisture content to maximize crop yields, creative uses for data gathered from space abound.

The international insurance company Swiss Re, for example, has signed a deal with Earth observation startup Iceye as part of its mission to close the insurance protection gap. "Using Iceye," says Pranav Pasricha, a senior Swiss Re executive, "we can quickly and accurately assess the extent of flooding, calculate loss estimates, and help our insurance clients [to] direct resources."

For decades, satellites have been an important tool for measuring our changing climate: Roughly 60% of the World Meteorological Organization's essential climate variables (physical, chemical, or biological variables critical to the Earth's climate) incorporate space-based data, and several variables can be measured only from space. Today a new generation of commercial satellites provide an array of targeted environmental data that is valuable to business leaders. From measuring a company's greenhouse gas emissions (GHGSat, Bluefield), to optimizing solar panel usage (Solargis), to measuring heat waste (Satellite Vu), to informing the measurement of ESG risks (Planet Labs with Moody's), commercial satellites are helping businesses measure their environmental impacts and meet their sustainability goals. Earth observation company Spire, which operates a fleet of small satellites, offers sophisticated weather prediction that helps companies make decisions about their operations. As Space Capital's report on climate asserts, "the need for persistent global monitoring and coordination will [make] every company of tomorrow . . . a space company."

As remote-sensing companies have matured, their products have evolved from raw data to "incredible products that are simple to use," according to Kevin Weil, the president of product and business at Planet Labs, a leading remote-sensing company. The biggest hurdle for these Earth observation companies? "Awareness," says Weil. "The data and the impact coming from Planet and the rest of the Earth observation industry could be 100 times what it is if there was more awareness." Advances in artificial intelligence and machine learning, incorporation of other data sources, and improvements in the satellite technologies themselves will only enhance the impact of space-based data.

The use of satellites as relay posts for data transmission is also growing. Although ground-based networks tend to be faster, as the data doesn't have to travel into space and back, the high cost of extending terrestrial infrastructure and the demand for mobile broadband have greatly increased interest in connecting to the internet through space.

In 2019 Bloomberg reported that Apple was considering building its own satellites to provide its devices with widespread internet coverage; in September, Apple announced the iPhone 14 will include built-in satellite connectivity for emergency communications. SpaceX has said that its cloud of Starlink satellites, when completed, could turn any spot on the globe into an internet hotspot—a capability that made headlines when Starlink helped assure internet access for Ukrainian leaders in the face of Russian aggression. In a matter of hours, SpaceX activated Starlink access in Ukraine and shipped terminals for use by the Ukrainian government. Starlink and other satellite-based broadband services, like Amazon's Project Kuiper, could significantly expand access to high-speed internet. As complementary infrastructure and products are developed, such as SatixFy's recently announced aircraft-mounted terminal designed to provide highly reliable broadband to airline passengers, space-based internet will offer consumers and businesses attractive new possibilities.

## Capabilities: Using the Unique Characteristics of Space

Executives should also ask, What value can my company create from activities conducted in space? While this may sound more like science fiction than current business reality, experiments that will shape many terrestrial industries in the future are already in progress.

Pharmaceutical companies, for example, are using the low-gravity vacuum of space to support cutting-edge R&D. Bristol Myers Squibb is a case in point. Since 1995 the company has collaborated with BioServe to conduct outer space experiments on fungal and bacterial fermentation, medicinal plant growth, and X-ray crystallography on the International Space Station (ISS). Similarly, Merck has been sending payloads to the ISS since 2014 to study the development of crystals in their drugs. This research hopes to improve drug manufacturing and storage.

Pharma companies aren't the only ones using space capabilities for research. Experiments in the microgravity environment of Earth's orbit have contributed to our understanding of fluid physics, the structures of gels and pastes (colloids), muscle atrophy and bone loss, combustion, and much more, with applications for health care, manufacturing, and many other industries. Experiments in space biology have generated insights about plants' growth and germination in microgravity, for example, and their responses to light. Research like this has commercial implications for the future of the agriculture and food industries.

Beyond R&D, many companies are working to usher in a new era of manufacturing that uses the unique environment of space. Companies such as Made In Space (part of Redwire) and Varda plan to build in space, eliminating the need to design satellites and other space infrastructure to survive the violent launch process. Doing so would open up entirely new possibilities for the shape, functionality, and cost of space assets.

For example, Made In Space and other companies are working on products such as ZBLAN, which is a fluoride glass fiber that is potentially 20 times more efficient than traditional fiber-optic cables. ZBLAN is difficult to produce on Earth, but its in-orbit production is a possible first step in manufacturing it at scale in space, for Earth. Or consider LambdaVision, which is pursuing synthetic retina manufacturing in orbit, and Maana Electric, which is developing a terrestrial solar-panel manufacturing process that could work on the moon. In addition, nearly a dozen firms are cooperating on designs—four of which have received more than $100 million each in funding from NASA—for commercial space stations to be completed later this decade. These new stations are designed to attract private R&D, manufacturing, and other sources of demand, like tourists. When completed, they will make it easier and more valuable than ever to operate in space.

Manufacturing in space has been a goal for decades. But the dramatic decline in launch costs for raw-material inputs, coupled with the promised efficiency of stations designed for it, are changing its economic viability for the better. The same forces of lower costs and greater functionality that have spurred dramatic growth in the satellite sector are now coming into play in in-space capabilities.

## Resources: Utilizing Space Assets

As humans expand their operations in space, they will increasingly look to use resources found in space. The earliest ventures in this area will likely target the moon; 70 commercial lunar missions have already been planned for the next 10 years. For example, Orbit Fab is building an "in-space propellant supply chain" that could tap water resources on the moon to stock its "gas stations in space," making possible the refueling and repositioning of satellites and satellite servicing systems.

Looking beyond the moon, additive manufacturing specialist Relativity Space foresees using its cutting-edge technology—which today it applies to building rockets—to construct an "industrial base" on Mars. Even more broadly, Jeff Bezos has stated that part of the vision behind Blue Origin is "to take all heavy industry, all polluting industry, and move it into space. And keep Earth as this beautiful gem of a planet that it is."

It's hard to predict how quickly in-situ resource utilization will develop because we are still so early in the rise of the space economy. And while the early glow of startups such as Planetary Resources and Deep Space Industries, which proposed mining valuable metals, water, and minerals from asteroids, faded when the market failed to develop rapidly enough, the sheer magnitude of mineral wealth available off-world will continue to attract interest. In May 2022, the startup AstroForge raised $13 million, and it's betting that the time is right to make asteroid mining a reality.

## Markets: Meeting Demand from the New Space Age

In the long term, companies will start to operate in space not simply because costs have fallen but also because the presence of more people in space, for longer periods, and more frequently, will generate demand for goods and services for consumption there.

Some of the markets will come from public-sector programs—NASA's Artemis program is designed to help establish sustained activity on the moon, for instance—but there is no better example of this than the rapidly developing interest in space tourism, a market expected to reach roughly $400 million in the next decade. Blue Origin and SpaceX have already taken paying passengers into space. As costs decline and technical infrastructure is assembled in orbit, other types of companies in the tourist sector will start to explore opportunities. Who will provide accommodation for space tourists? What kinds of activities will they be interested in?

On their heels will come commercial real-estate developers, lawyers, construction firms, and other players who specialize in creating hospitable and economically thriving terrestrial environments. Architects, designers, and artists will be asked to humanize the new spaces. In fact, some already have: When envisioning the habitation module for its planned space station, Axiom Space turned to industrial architect Philippe Starck, whose design evokes a nurturing, nestlike feeling (as well as offering a stunning view, of course). The construction firm Icon and the architecture firm the Bjarke Ingels Group have recently worked with NASA to help plan its construction system for the Artemis mission to the moon and create a structure called Mars Dune Alpha to simulate what it would be like to live on Mars.

If in the long run commercial habitats proliferate, perhaps even to the creation by 2050 of the city on Mars forecast by Elon Musk, then humans will want to enjoy their time in space. They will bring demands for all the creature comforts we have on Earth and for new experiences possible only in space. That is the sort of demand that markets are excellent at supplying. Substantial growth of the space-for-space economy will create opportunities akin to new geographic markets for firms of all types. While people sometimes lament that the expansion of global brands to all corners of the world has flattened experience, the operational excellence and reliable quality of global brands will provide welcome comfort in the harsh reaches of space.

Now let's look at how companies interested in capitalizing on one or more of these four areas of space value should get started.

## Be Ready to Fail Fast

Traditionally, exploiting a new market opportunity in tech has required would-be suppliers to be early movers—assembling the skills, resources, and capabilities to create new-to-the-world products and services. Is the same true for space? To answer this question, it's worth revisiting the history of the first wave of commercial space ventures.

In the fall of 1998, Iridium, a provider of global telephony services to consumers and businesses, announced the launch of its commercial service. Over the prior decade, Iridium had developed and launched a constellation of 75 satellites (66 for operations and nine spares) at a cost of more than $5 billion. That was a glittering achievement. No one had ever before assembled such a vast array of satellites in low-Earth orbit. And Iridium's satellites had capabilities that others did not—they talked to one another while whizzing around the globe at 17,000 miles per hour.

At launch, however, there were challenges with the technology, especially with the ability to make and receive calls in cities and inside buildings. More critically, the anticipated market failed to materialize. After five months, only 10,000 subscribers had signed up. Bleeding cash, and with too few customers to cover operating costs, Iridium filed for bankruptcy less than 10 months after launch.

# The cost and quantity of space ventures

*Falling launch costs have been accompanied by a rising number of active satellites over the past six decades.*

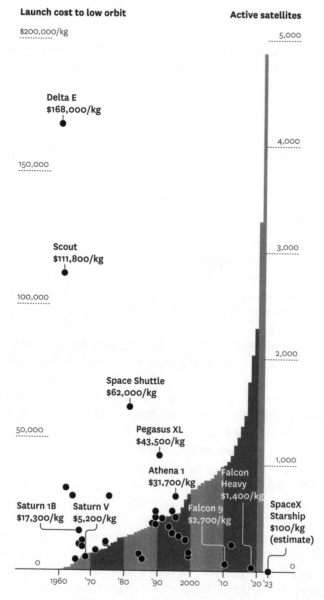

Launch cost to low orbit

$200,000/kg

Active satellites

5,000

Delta E
$168,000/kg

4,000

150,000

Scout
$111,800/kg

3,000

100,000

Space Shuttle
$62,000/kg

2,000

Pegasus XL
$43,500/kg

50,000

1,000

Athena 1
$31,700/kg

Falcon
Heavy
$1,400/kg

Saturn 1B          Saturn V
$17,300/kg       $5,200/kg

Falcon 9
$2,700/kg

SpaceX
Starship
$100/kg
(estimate)

0                                                                        0

1960      '70      '80      '90      2000      '10      '20  '23

*Source:* International Conference on Environmental Systems; Dr. Jonathan C. McDowell

Contrast this approach with Lynk, a venture with a similar goal: providing "fill-in" global cellular coverage that uses a customer's existing equipment. While Lynk's plans eventually required hundreds of satellites, they began with a series of experiments. Each experiment gave Lynk more information on the feasibility, desirability, and viability of the overall venture—and more information with which to plan the next experiment. In 2020 Lynk tested whether cell phones could receive a text from a single satellite in orbit and confirmed the system's technical feasibility. Then in 2022, with its fifth satellite, it tested two-way connectivity between space and earthbound equipment in five locations around the globe. During that test, the company received pings requesting service from thousands of regular user devices out of range of traditional cell towers, giving it an indication of potential demand. No one can know for certain whether Lynk will succeed in an increasingly crowded field. But its experiment-as-you-go philosophy allows for maximum flexibility to learn and adapt over time.

A flexible approach is beginning to dominate. In the early days of the space industry, government actors embarked on multibillion-dollar projects with elaborate processes for managing risk; failure was to be avoided at almost all costs. Now SpaceX and other startups have adopted the fail-fast approach common to the tech sector. As one executive remarked to a group of MBA students while watching a Starship systems test come to an explosive end: "Just think how much they learned from that test. If they had tried to eliminate that risk, it would have taken many more years and millions more dollars." As we prepare to enter the New Space Age, the message is clear. Space companies of the future can't avoid risk. They must embrace it and let it drive their learning.

## Find the Right Team

Space is not only an expensive business, it is also a highly complex one. As Dylan Taylor, cofounder and CEO of Voyager Space Holdings, says, "You capture value in space by [having] Capability A, marrying it with Capability B, and unlocking a new Capability C that's higher up on the food chain." That's why Voyager has acquired majority stakes in a range of space-focused companies covering launch, robotics, in-space manufacturing and research, travel, and more.

Of course not all companies can afford to use M&A to pursue space opportunities. In that case the best approach is to partner up. You'll be in good company. In December 2021, NASA awarded more than $400 million in contracts for commercial space-station development. All three winners were teams: Blue Origin partnered with Sierra Space, Boeing, Redwire, Genesis Engineering, and Arizona State University; Nanoracks partnered with Voyager Space and Lockheed Martin; and Northrop Grumman partnered with Dynetics, with more partners to be announced.

It's not just space-focused companies and space agencies that team up: Newcomers to space are also using partnerships to explore its potential. T-Mobile has partnered with SpaceX to allow their customers to send texts or make calls via satellite when no cell towers are available, eliminating "dead zones" in the United States. General Motors is working with Lockheed Martin to develop lunar rovers as part of the Artemis program. Caterpillar has partnered with NASA to advance technologies and equipment for remote 3D printing of space habitats from material found on Mars.

In addition, partnerships can be built to suit different levels of engagement. You may want to start by simply monitoring the activities of companies in the space economy that are likely to need your firm's capabilities. Becoming a limited partner in a space-focused fund, for example, could give you a window into the sector and a network to help you build knowledge and relationships.

If you have an idea for a good or service you could produce or provide in space if a key partnership could be developed, make that partnership happen. Initiate exploratory discussions with companies working in space to identify mutually beneficial partnerships. It's even worth your time to talk with companies that you suspect may turn to space soon. Axiom, Nanoracks, Spire, and many others are eager to connect with potential customers and partners to identify new applications for their capabilities.

Finally, consider tapping into the resources—financial, organizational, and technical—offered by space agencies around the world. NASA, the European Space Agency, the Japan Aerospace Exploration Agency, the Indian Space Research Organisation, and others can be powerful partners and facilitators of commercial partnerships. Roughly 90% of the first $1 billion invested in SpaceX came from NASA's contracting arrangements, bringing some predictability to an inherently risky venture. Today space agencies are expanding their dealings with the commercial sector, creating interesting business opportunities in space and on Earth. For instance, to develop lunar rovers, NASA is collaborating with GM and Goodyear, and JAXA has separate partnerships with Toyota and Nissan. About a third of patents filed in the United States depend on publicly funded R&D, and these are a lot more valuable than patents that don't. Companies, especially those just getting started in space, would do well to reach out to these public-sector actors as well as those in the national security sector. They can provide valuable seed funding, advice for navigating complex regulatory environments, and hard-won lessons from their experience in space.

---

It took almost a century before the automobile achieved dominance in transportation, and automotive technology underwent many changes in that time. The first cars were little more than glorified electric go-karts and, despite the development of lead batteries, were limited in range and speed. It wasn't until the advent of the internal combustion engine that cars' potential became clear. The space industry will develop in similar ways—with uneven progress and unexpected technological twists.

Like all industries, the space business will experience downs as well as ups. In the near term, as economies grapple with the threat of recession, the commitment of VC and other funds will certainly be reduced. Already there is talk of a space bubble ready to burst. The space industry will surely go through periods of consolidation and retrenchment, as weaker players drop out or are acquired by rivals.

Once a tipping point is reached, though, private engagement can deliver progress at great speed as entrepreneurs resolve remaining challenges. It's true that some of the deliverables may be decades or even centuries in the future. But right now the $300 billion and growing satellite industry is poised to revolutionize an array of sectors through data and connectivity, capitalizing on designs and scale made possible by falling launch costs and advances in technology. With the immense opportunity available today, it's time to start thinking about your company's strategy for space.

**Originally published in November–December 2022. Reprint** R2206E

# Democratizing Transformation

*by Marco Iansiti and Satya Nadella*

**OVER THE PAST DECADE**, Novartis has invested heavily in digital transformation. As the Swiss pharmaceutical giant moved its technology infrastructure to the cloud and invested in data platforms and data integration, it recruited AI specialists and data scientists to build machine-learning models and deploy them throughout the firm. But even as the technical teams grew, managers from across the business—sales, supply chain, HR, finance, and marketing—weren't embracing the newly available information, nor were they thinking much about how data could enhance their teams' work. At the same time, the data scientists had little visibility into the business units and could not easily integrate data into day-to-day operations. As a result, the investments resulted in only occasional successes (in some aspects of the R&D process, for example) while many pilots and projects sputtered.

More recently, however, pilots targeting both R&D and marketing personalization started showing business value and captured the attention and imagination of some of Novartis's more creative business executives. They became increasingly excited about opportunities to deploy AI in various parts of the company and began to earnestly champion the efforts. (Disclosure: We have both worked with Novartis and other companies mentioned in this article in a variety of ways, including board membership, research, and consulting.) They realized that technologists and data scientists alone couldn't bring about the kind of wholesale innovation the business needed, so they began pairing data scientists with business employees who had insight into where improvements in efficiency and performance were needed.

Novartis also invested in training frontline business employees to use data themselves to drive innovation. A growing number of teams adopted agile methods to address all kinds of opportunities. The intensity and impact of transformation thus accelerated rapidly, driving a range of innovation initiatives, including digitally enabling sales and sales forecasting, reconceiving the order and replenishment system for health-care-services customers, and revamping prescription-fulfillment systems and processes.

The progress in digital transformation became invaluable as the company dealt with the initial chaos of the pandemic. Novartis business teams partnered with data scientists to devise models to manage supply-chain disruptions, predict shortages of critical supplies, and enable quick changes to product mix and pricing policies. They also developed analytics to identify patients who were at risk because they were putting off doctor visits. As the Covid crisis wore on, the value of AI became obvious to managers companywide.

Before this wave of AI adoption, Novartis's investments in technology consisted almost entirely of packaged enterprise applications, usually implemented by the IT department with the guidance of external consultants, vendors, or systems integrators. But to build companywide digital capability, under the leadership of then chief digital officer Bertrand Bodson, Novartis not only developed new capabilities in data science but also started to democratize access to data and technology well outside traditional tech silos. The company is now training employees at all levels and in all functions to identify and capitalize on opportunities for incorporating data and technology to improve their work. In 2021, the Novartis yearly AI summit was attended by thousands of employees.

The potential for employee-driven digital innovation is impossible to calculate, but according to the market research firm IDC's Worldwide IT Industry 2020 Predictions report, enterprises across the global economy will need to create some 500 million new

# Idea in Brief

## The Problem

Many companies struggle to reap the benefits of investments in digital transformation, while others see enormous gains. What do successful companies do differently?

## The Journey

This article describes the five stages of digital transformation, from the traditional stage, where digital and technology are the province of the IT department, through to the platform stage, where a comprehensive

software foundation enables the rapid deployment of AI-based applications.

## The Ideal

The ideal is the native stage, whose hallmarks are an operating architecture designed to deploy AI at scale across a huge, distributed spectrum of applications; a core of experts; broadly accessible, easy-to-use tools; and investment in training and capability-building among large groups of business-people.

digital solutions by 2023—more than the total number created over the past 40 years. This cannot be accomplished by small groups of technologists and data scientists walled off in organizational silos. It will require much larger and more-diverse groups of employees—executives, managers, and frontline workers—coming together to rethink how every aspect of the business should operate. Our research sheds light on how to do that.

## The Success Drivers

When we started our research, we wanted to understand why many companies struggle to reap the benefits of investments in digital transformation while others see enormous gains. What do successful companies do differently?

We looked at 150 companies in manufacturing, health care, consumer products, financial services, aerospace, and pharma/biotech, including a representative sample of the largest firms in each sector. Some were failing to move the needle, but many had made dramatic progress. Perhaps surprisingly, we found that outcomes did not depend on the relative size of IT budgets. Nor were the success stories confined to "born digital" organizations. Legacy giants such as Unilever, Fidelity, and Starbucks (where one of us, Satya, is on the board)—not to mention Novartis—had managed to create a digital innovation mindset and culture.

Our research shows that to enable transformation at scale, companies must create synergy in three areas:

## Capabilities

Successful transformation efforts require that companies develop digital and data skills in employees outside traditional technology functions. These capabilities alone, however, are not sufficient to deliver the full benefits of transformation; organizations must also invest in developing process agility and, more broadly, a culture that encourages widespread, frequent experimentation.

## Technology

Of course, investment in the right technologies is important, especially in the elements of an AI stack: data platform technology, data engineering, machine-learning algorithms, and algorithm-deployment technology. Companies must ensure that the technology deployed is easy to use and accessible to the many nontechnical employees participating in innovation efforts.

## Architecture

Investment in organizational and technical architecture is necessary to ensure that human capabilities and technology can work in synergy to drive innovation. That requires an architecture—for both technology and the organization—that supports the sharing, integration, and normalization of data (for example, making data definitions and characteristics consistent) across traditionally isolated silos. This is the only real, scalable way to assemble the necessary technological and data assets so that they are available to a distributed workforce.

Many large companies are making headway in each of these areas. But even leading companies tend to underestimate the importance of getting employees to pull transformation into their functions

# The Elements of Tech Intensity

**TO ENABLE TRANSFORMATION,** companies must create synergy in three key areas:

## Capabilities

- Organizational culture
- Training and development
- Low-code/no-code tools
- Agile teams
- Organizational architecture
- Citizen developers
- Product management

## Technology

- Machine learning
- Deep learning
- DevOps pipelines
- Data encryption
- Real-time analytics

## Architecture

- Data platform
- Horizontal integration and normalization
- Data documentation
- API strategy
- Experimentation and risk
- Data governance

and their work rather than having central technology groups and consultants push the changes out to the business. As Eric von Hippel of MIT has advocated for many years, frontline users, who are closest to the use cases and best positioned to develop solutions that fit

## Digital transformation pays off

*We studied 150 companies in a range of industries and found that revenue growth and compound annual growth rate among the leaders (the top quartile) in tech intensity were more than double that of the laggards (the bottom quartile).*

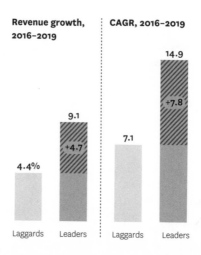

**Revenue growth, 2016–2019**

4.4%
9.1 (+4.7)

**CAGR, 2016–2019**

7.1
14.9 (+7.8)

Laggards    Leaders    Laggards    Leaders

*Source:* Keystone

their needs, must take a central role, joining agile teams that dynamically coalesce and dissolve on the basis of business needs.

## Building Tech Intensity

Our research unpacks how capabilities, technology, and architecture work together to build what we call *tech intensity.* Derived from the economics concept of intensive margin—how much a resource is utilized or applied—tech intensity refers to the extent to which employees put technology to use to drive digital innovation and achieve business outcomes. Our research found that companies that made good investments in technology and made tools accessible to a broad community of data- and tech-skilled employees achieved higher tech intensity—and superior performance. Companies that failed to develop tech- and data-related capabilities in their employees and offered only limited access to technology were left behind.

We ranked the tech intensity of the 150 firms in our study and found that the top quartile of the sample grew their revenues more than twice as fast as the bottom quartile. (See the exhibit "Digital transformation pays off." To score your firm's tech intensity, go to www.keystone.ai/techintensity.) We also found that technology, capability, and architecture indices correlated with other measures of performance, from productivity and profits to growth in enterprise value. Using an econometric technique known as *instrumental variables,* we also found evidence that the relationship between tech intensity and performance was causal: That is, greater intensity (especially investments in technical and organizational architecture) powered higher revenue growth.

## Staging the Transformation

Our analysis confirms that just spending money on technology does not result in more growth or better performance; in fact, in some cases it can actually damage the business if it accentuates divisions and inconsistencies across groups. Instead, it is the architectural, managerial, and organizational approaches to transformation that best explain the substantial and enduring differences among firms. We found that companies typically progress through five stages on their transformation journey. (See the exhibit "The stages of digital maturity.")

### Traditional model
Not surprisingly, many companies fit what we consider to be the traditional model of digital innovation, whereby digital and technology investments are the province of the IT department (or other technical specialist groups) and impact is scattered across groups, mostly in inconsistent ways. IT works with business units to fund projects and

## The stages of digital maturity

*Digital maturity is made up of these characteristics of organizational structure, process, tech architecture, and tech deployment. How does your company stack up?*

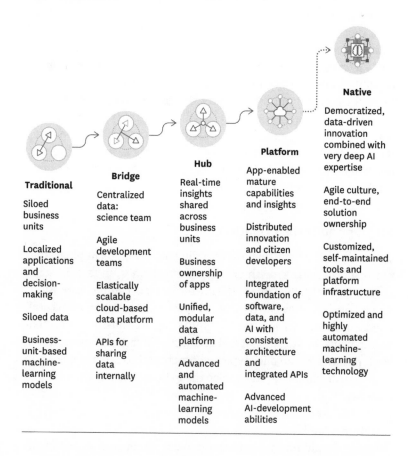

**Native**

Democratized, data-driven innovation combined with very deep AI expertise

Agile culture, end-to-end solution ownership

Customized, self-maintained tools and platform infrastructure

Optimized and highly automated machine-learning technology

**Platform**

App-enabled mature capabilities and insights

Distributed innovation and citizen developers

Integrated foundation of software, data, and AI with consistent architecture and integrated APIs

Advanced AI-development abilities

**Hub**

Real-time insights shared across business units

Business ownership of apps

Unified, modular data platform

Advanced and automated machine-learning models

**Bridge**

Centralized data: science team

Agile development teams

Elastically scalable cloud-based data platform

APIs for sharing data internally

**Traditional**

Siloed business units

Localized applications and decision-making

Siloed data

Business-unit-based machine-learning models

manage implementation—say, for the deployment of an enterprise application or a data platform technology. The projects and their implementations are customized to the specific requirements of the individual silos, business units, or functions. The result is that over time, the technology and data infrastructure reflect the quirks of individual groups, without any consistency and connectivity. This sort of disjointed approach makes it virtually impossible to share, scale, or distribute innovation efforts across the organization.

Many businesses in the traditional model still spend a great deal of money on information technology. Consider a financial services firm we studied, whose tech and analytics budget is among the top in its industry, in both absolute and relative terms. The company has spent heavily on state-of-the-art data-platform technology and hired thousands of IT specialists and data scientists, who sit isolated in a separate IT group, while few (if any) employees on the business side are involved in the organization's digital innovation efforts. The company thus lacks the architecture and capabilities required to foster any intensity in tech adoption. Not surprisingly, the firm's IT and data sciences efforts have stalled, and business impact has been minimal.

A telltale sign that a company is in the traditional stage is that perceptions of impact among technology and business employees are dramatically different. The former perceive impact to be high (as measured by the effort they put into their work), while the latter measure it as much lower (according to how their everyday activities have benefited).

### Bridge model

To break free of the traditional constraints of silos—organizational and infrastructural—companies typically start by launching pilots that bridge previously separate groups and developing shareable data and technology assets to enable new innovations. They might first focus on specific functional opportunities such as optimizing advertising, manufacturing, or supply-chain capabilities. These companies are piloting not only technology but also a fundamentally different model of innovation in which executives, managers, and frontline workers from the business side work in collaboration with IT and data scientists. Victor Bulto, Novartis's head of U.S. pharmaceuticals, was instrumental in launching early pilots (focusing, for example, on identifying at-risk patients) and served as

## Digital maturity by industry

*We looked at 150 companies in a range of industries and plotted the average levels of technology capability and technology architecture for each industry. Companies in consumer packaged goods, for example, tended to be at the early stage of the transformation journey; aerospace and health-care firms were much more advanced.*

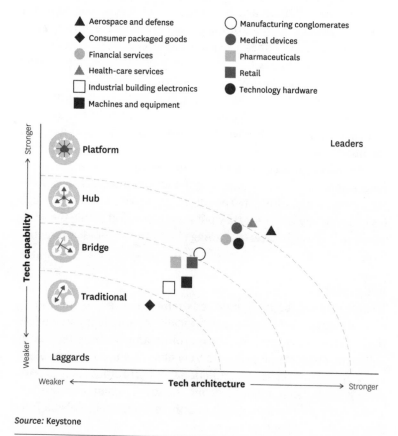

*Source:* Keystone

a champion for many initiatives as the organization moved through the bridge stage. Lori Beer, JPMorgan Chase's global CIO, likes to talk about the demonstrated impact of piloting AI to simplify expense reporting and approval—a process-improvement pilot that won over many employees.

## Hubs

As more and more pilots demonstrate the success of the new approach, organizations form data and capability hubs and gradually develop the capacity to link and engage additional functions and business units in pursuit of opportunities for transformation. As they progress down this path, leaders begin to realize that the bottleneck in innovation has shifted from investments in technology to investments in the workforce. The limiting factor at this stage is the number of business employees with the capability—the know-how and the access—to drive digital innovation. Companies thus need to invest in coaching and training a much larger community of employees.

Fidelity strives to develop what it calls *digital athletes*. It began to build hubs by creating centralized data assets (a companywide data lake, for example); now it is scaling up training for thousands of business employees, giving them the capacity to deploy digitally enabled solutions across the entire business. Digitally savvy investment specialists and tax experts, for example, are working closely with data scientists and technologists to create innovative solutions with a special focus on personalization and tailored customer impact. They've also created an app aimed at onboarding and engaging younger investors and another app for delivering AI-powered recommendations to Fidelity financial advisers, to name just a few examples.

Starbucks, too, is focused not only on technology and architecture but also on developing broad-based, agile innovation skills in its employees to power its hubs. CEO Kevin Johnson explains, "We've gone from large teams working in silos to smaller, cross-functional teams [everywhere], and from evaluating every idea as pass-fail to rapid iteration." Starbucks is now a digital innovation powerhouse, with sophisticated customer apps enabling remote ordering, loyalty programs, and payment systems along with internal systems enabling AI-based labor allocation and inventory management.

## Platform model

As companies enter the platform stage, data hubs merge into a comprehensive software foundation that enables the rapid deployment of AI-based applications. Firms focus on building sophisticated data-engineering capabilities and encouraging the reuse and integration of machine-learning models. Analytics-based prediction models are applied across the business, with an increasing focus on the automation of basic operational tasks. Organizations begin to function a bit more like software companies, developing comprehensive capabilities that enable product and program management and rapid experimentation.

Over the past five years, Microsoft has gone through almost every stage of this journey. Years ago, we were just as siloed as most companies, with each product-based organization segregating its own data, software, and capabilities. As we connected and normalized data from different functions and product groups, we were able to deploy integrated solutions in areas ranging from customer service to supply-chain management.

We integrated all our data in a companywide data lake, and we built what we call a *business process platform,* which provides software and analytics components that teams use to enable innovation in areas ranging from Xbox manufacturing to managing advertising spend. We also invested in training programs for nontechnical employees, cultivating data-centric and machine-learning capabilities throughout the organization.

## Native model

The most successful companies among the 150 in our study have deployed an entirely different type of operating architecture, centered on integrated data assets and software libraries and designed to deploy AI at scale across a huge, distributed spectrum of applications. Its hallmarks are a core of experts; broadly accessible, easy-to-use tools; and investment in training and capability-building among large groups of businesspeople. These companies are approaching the capacity of digital natives such as Airbnb and Uber, which were purpose-built to scale companywide analytics and software-based innovation. Airbnb and Uber are certainly not perfect, but they come close to the native ideal.

At Microsoft, we still have a lot to learn, but in some parts of the organization we are starting to approach the native model. As is common in any enterprise, the progress has not been uniform. Different groups have achieved different levels of capability, but the results overall are encouraging, as we see increasingly innovative solutions to internal and customer-facing problems. Most critically, our companywide approach to understanding, protecting, and working with data has progressed by light years.

## The Imperative for Leaders

The mandate for digital transformation creates a leadership imperative: Embrace transformation, and work to sustain it. Articulate a clear strategy and communicate it relentlessly. Establish an organizational architecture to evolve into as you make the myriad daily decisions that define your technology strategy. Deploy a real governance process to track the many technology projects underway, and coordinate and integrate them whenever possible. Champion agility in all business initiatives you touch and influence. And finally, break free of tradition. Train and coach your employees to understand the potential of technology and data, and release the innovators within your workforce.

This mandate extends to technology providers. Despite much investment, technologies are still too complex and are often too hard to use and deploy. We need tools and technology that make driving transformation intuitive for frontline workers while keeping data secure. Let's not forget that until recently many of us were relying on specialists in Fortran and Cobol to model business problems and even to perform basic mathematical operations. Spreadsheets brought about a revolution in mathematical modeling; we need technology providers to bring the same revolution to AI and make using a machine-learning application as easy as creating a pivot table.

Momentum is growing. But we must sustain the efforts to ensure that companies of all stripes make it across the digital divide.

**Originally published in May–June 2022.  Reprint** S22031

# About the Contributors

**PRITHWIRAJ (RAJ) CHOUDHURY** is the Lumry Family Associate Professor at Harvard Business School. He was an assistant professor at Wharton prior to joining Harvard. His research is focused on studying the future of work, especially the changing geography of work. In particular, he studies the productivity effects of geographic mobility of workers, causes of geographic immobility, and productivity effects of remote work practices such as "work from anywhere" and "all remote."

**KRISTI DePAUL** is a content creator whose writing on career navigation and personal branding has appeared in international outlets and has been cited by prominent think tanks and universities. She is founder and principal at Nuanced, a thought leadership firm for executives, and serves as CEO of Founders, a fully remote content agency focused on the future of learning and the future of work. She earned a master's degree from the H. John Heinz III College of Information Systems and Public Policy at Carnegie Mellon University.

**BRANDON FOGEL** is a doctoral student at the University of Nebraska–Lincoln. He is a coauthor of *Gentelligence: The Revolutionary Approach to Leading an Intergenerational Workforce*.

**JOSEPH FULLER** is a professor of management practice and a cochair of the Managing the Future of Work project at Harvard Business School. He also cochairs the Harvard Project on the Workforce, a collaboration among members of the faculty at the university's schools of business, education, and government.

**MEGAN W. GERHARDT** is a professor of management and the director of leadership development at the Farmer School of Business at Miami University, as well as the Robert D. Johnson Codirector of the school's William Isaac and Michael Oxley Center for Business Leadership. She is a coauthor of *Gentelligence: The Revolutionary Approach to Leading an Intergenerational Workforce*.

**DIANE GHERSON** is the former chief human resources officer of IBM and a senior lecturer of business administration at Harvard Business School.

**LYNDA GRATTON** is a professor of management practice at London Business School and the founder of HSM Advisory, the future-of-work research consultancy. Her most recent book is *Redesigning Work: How to Transform Your Organization and Make Hybrid Work for Everyone.*

**STEPHEN HANSEN** is an associate professor of economics at Imperial College Business School.

**MARCO IANSITI** is the David Sarnoff Professor of Business Administration at Harvard Business School, where he heads the Technology and Operations Management Unit and the Digital Initiative. He has advised many companies in the technology sector, including Microsoft, Facebook, and Amazon. He is a coauthor (with Karim Lakhani) of the book *Competing in the Age of AI* (Harvard Business Review Press, 2020).

**TARUN KHANNA** is the Jorge Paulo Lemann Professor at Harvard Business School, the director of Harvard's Lakshmi Mittal South Asia Institute, and the author of *Trust: Creating the Foundation for Entrepreneurship in Developing Countries.*

**MARK R. KRAMER** is a senior lecturer at Harvard Business School. He is also a cofounder of the social impact consulting firm FSG and a partner at the impact investing hedge fund at Congruence Capital.

**ALAN MacCORMACK** is the MBA Class of 1949 Adjunct Professor of Business Administration at Harvard Business School. He is an expert in the management of innovation and new product development and a core faculty member in the MS/MBA joint degree program with the School of Engineering and Applied Sciences.

**JOSEPHINE NACHEMSON-EKWALL** is vice president, independent compliance and risk management, at Citi. She is a coauthor of *Gentelligence: The Revolutionary Approach to Leading an Intergenerational Workforce.*

**SATYA NADELLA** is the chairman and CEO of Microsoft.

**PJ NEAL** is the global head of knowledge and operations for the Board & CEO Advisory Group at Russell Reynolds Associates.

**SUSAN PEPPERCORN** is an executive career transition coach and speaker. She is the author of *Ditch Your Inner Critic at Work: Evidence-Based Strategies to Thrive in Your Career.*

**MARC W. PFITZER** is a managing director at FSG, a global social-impact consulting firm.

**KARTHIK RAMANNA** is a professor of business and public policy at Oxford University's Blavatnik School of Government. He is a coauthor (with Robert S. Kaplan) of the 2022 McKinsey Award–winning article "Accounting for Climate Change" (*Harvard Business Review*, November–December 2021).

**THOMAS S. ROBERTSON,** the former dean of The Wharton School, is the Joshua J. Harris Professor of Marketing and the academic director of the Jay H. Baker Retailing Center at Wharton.

**STEVEN G. ROGELBERG** holds the title of the Chancellor's Professor at the University of North Carolina at Charlotte for his distinguished national, international, and interdisciplinary contributions. He is also the author of *The Surprising Science of Meetings: How You Can Lead Your Team to Peak Performance* and *Glad We Met: The Art and Science of 1:1 Meetings*. He writes and speaks about leadership, teams, meetings, and engagement. Follow him on LinkedIn or find more information at stevenrogelberg.com.

**BRENDAN ROSSEAU** is a research associate and teaching fellow at Harvard Business School.

**RAFFAELLA SADUN** is the Charles E. Wilson Professor of Business Administration at Harvard Business School.

**VASUNDHARA SAWHNEY** is a senior editor at *Harvard Business Review*.

**THOMAS STACKPOLE** is a senior editor at *Harvard Business Review*.

**ELLA F. WASHINGTON** is an organizational psychologist; the founder and CEO of Ellavate Solutions, a DEI strategy firm; a professor of practice at Georgetown University's McDonough School of Business; and a cohost of Gallup's Center on Black Voices *Cultural Competence* podcast. She is the author of *The Necessary Journey: Making Real Progress on Equity and Inclusion* (Harvard Business Review Press, 2022).

**MATTHEW WEINZIERL** is the Joseph and Jacqueline Elbling Professor of Business Administration at Harvard Business School and a research associate at the National Bureau of Economic Research. His teaching and research focus on the design of economic policy and the economics and business of space.

**MOLLY WHITE** is a software developer and Wikipedia editor.

**LILY ZHENG** is a diversity, equity, and inclusion strategist, consultant, and speaker who works with organizations to achieve the DEI impact and outcomes they need. They are the author of *DEI Deconstructed: Your No-Nonsense Guide to Doing the Work and Doing it Right*.

# Index

# Engage with HBR content the way you want, on any device.

With HBR's subscription plans, you can access world-renowned case studies from Harvard Business School and receive four **free eBooks**. Download and customize prebuilt **slide decks and graphics** from our **Data & Visuals** collection. With HBR's archive, top 50 best-selling articles, and five new articles every day, HBR is more than just a magazine.

Subscribe Today
**HBR.org/success**

# The most important management ideas all in one place.

We hope you enjoyed this book from *Harvard Business Review*. Now you can get even more with HBR's 10 Must Reads Boxed Set. From books on leadership and strategy to managing yourself and others, this 6-book collection delivers articles on the most essential business topics to help you succeed.

## HBR's 10 Must Reads Series

**The definitive collection of ideas and best practices on our most sought-after topics from the best minds in business.**

- Change Management
- Collaboration
- Communication
- Emotional Intelligence
- Innovation
- Leadership
- Making Smart Decisions
- Managing Across Cultures
- Managing People
- Managing Yourself
- Strategic Marketing
- Strategy
- Teams
- The Essentials

hbr.org/mustreads